MOJANG STUDIOS

MINECRAFT

MATHS

OFFICIAL WORKBOOK

AGES 9-10

DAN LIPSCOMBE AND

KATHERINE PATE

INTRODUCTION

HOW TO USE THIS BOOK

Welcome to an exciting educational experience! Your child will go on a series of adventures through the amazing world of Minecraft, improving their maths skills along the way. Matched to the National Curriculum for maths for ages 9–10 (Year 5), this workbook takes your child into fascinating landscapes where our heroes Rosa and Isaac embark on building projects and daring treasure hunts…all while keeping those pesky mobs at bay!

As each adventure unfolds, your child will complete topic-based questions worth a certain number of emeralds . These can then be 'traded in' on the final page. The more challenging questions are marked with this icon to stretch your child's learning. Answers are included at the back of the book.

MEET OUR HEROES

Rosa experiments with machines and redstone. If ever a minecart track or piston machine is needed, Rosa will know how to make it work. She keeps trying to work out how Nether portals work, but always ends up pulled through to the other dimension! Rosa loves slimes because slimeballs are used to craft sticky pistons. If she could keep one as a pet, she would!

Isaac enjoys learning, a lot. Whether it is science or geography, he will gobble up information. Rather than at home, he is often found exploring new places. He likes nothing more than wandering home with an inventory full of ingredients and spending the rest of the day brewing potions and testing them on his friends.

First published in 2021 by Collins
An imprint of HarperCollins*Publishers*
1 London Bridge Street, London, SE1 9GF

HarperCollins*Publishers*
1st Floor, Watermarque Building, Ringsend Road, Dublin 4, Ireland

Publisher: Fiona McGlade
Authors: Dan Lipscombe and Katherine Pate
Project management: Richard Toms
Design: Ian Wrigley and Sarah Duxbury
Typesetting: Nicola Lancashire at Rose and Thorn Creative Services

Special thanks to Alex Wiltshire, Sherin Kwan and Marie-Louise Bengtsson at Mojang and the team at Farshore

Production: Karen Nulty

ISBN: 978-0-00-846278-9

British Library Cataloguing in Publication Data.

A CIP record of this book is available from the British Library.

1 2 3 4 5 6 7 8 9 10

Printed in the United Kingdom

MIX
Paper from responsible source
FSC™ C007454

This book is produced from independently certified FSC™ paper to ensure responsible forest management.

For more information visit: www.harpercollins.co.uk/green

CONTENTS

NUMBER AND PLACE VALUE

STEPPING ON TO THE SAND

The desert is a rather barren place. Water, of course, is difficult to find and so are animals. Only light-coloured rabbits scamper through the sand dunes, looking for something to eat. Spiky cacti rise from the sand to prick those who come too close, but this plant can be harvested for making dye.

DESERT DANGER

The usual mobs of skeletons, spiders and creepers roam at night. Most zombies that spawn in deserts are the husk variant, which inflict the Hunger effect and don't burn in daylight.

LOOKING FOR LOOT

A hero wandering the sand can find safety in a village made of sandstone. Many deserts, just like this one, will hold loot for those brave enough to look for it. Finding a desert pyramid is key to this treasure hunt. Some say these were places of worship and where precious possessions could be hidden.

A TOUGH TREK

Our heroine Rosa has been walking for days. She left home some time ago, in search of new and interesting biomes. She ran out of food long ago. She hasn't brought a bed to rest in and so has been fighting all night. Just when she thinks about giving up, she sees something that gives her hope.

PLACE VALUE AND ROUNDING

Rosa is tired and hungry. In fact, she's so hungry that her health is running low. She must find something to eat soon. In the distance, she spots a sandstone structure with some coloured blocks in the wall.

1

Find the missing number in each sequence.

a) 57,893   67,893   77,893   87,893   *97,893*

b) 132,087   131,087   130,087   *129,087*   128,087

c) *779,952*   780,952   781,952   782,952   783,952

2

There is so much space out here in the desert! Rosa imagines that she could build a city made from **79,496** blocks.

Find the number that is:

a) 1 more   *79,497*

b) 10 more   *79,506*

c) 100 more   *79,596*

d) 1,000 more   *80,496*

e) 10,000 more   *89,496*

f) 100,000 more   *179,496*

3

a) Write fifty-one thousand, six hundred and twenty-seven in digits. *51,627*

b) Write 20,046 in words.   *twenty thousand and forty six*

As Rosa arrives at the building, she's relieved to find it is real and not a mirage. It's a desert pyramid and the coloured blocks make part of an image in the towers. Rosa wonders how much loot might be hidden inside.

4

Rosa makes six guesses about how many pieces of loot there might be. If you wrote these numbers in order, starting with the highest, which one would be 5th in the list?

Guess 1: 34,109	**Guess 2:** 39,184 _5th_	**Guess 3:** 44,119
Guess 4: 45,732	**Guess 5:** 39,189	**Guess 6:** 44,901

5

Write **<** or **>** in the boxes to make each statement correct.

a)   88,101 88,011

b)   973,183 973,193

Rosa wonders what 45,732 pieces of loot would look like. A huge treasure trove, that's for sure!

6

In the number **45,732** what is the value of:

a)   the digit 3?   _30_

b)   the digit 4?   _40,000_

c)   the digit 5?   _5,000_

7

Colour in the boxes that have numbers with 4 hundreds.

483,296	 1,392,482	 37,476	284,395	583,406.87

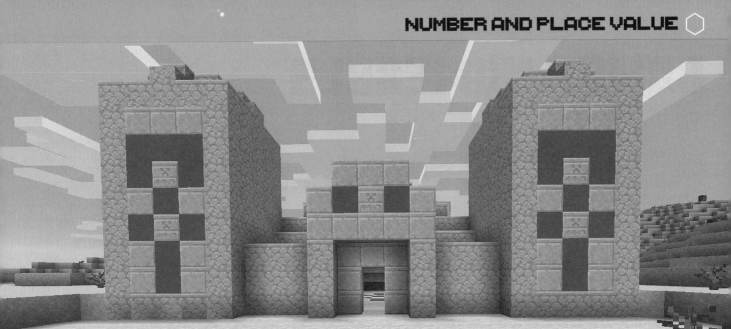

As Rosa enters the desert pyramid, an eerie silence falls. She has no idea where the loot might be, but the central area of the pyramid has a floor displaying a pattern made from orange terracotta. Rosa approaches the terracotta, with her pickaxe ready. As she gets to work, make sense of some more large numbers.

8

Round **804,763** to the nearest:

a) 100,000 ....

b) 10,000 ....

9

Round each number to the nearest ten thousand and give the estimated answer.

a) 68,651 − 23,425 ....

b) 74,453 + 40,464 ....

10

A number rounded to the nearest ten thousand is 30,000.

a) What is the largest whole number it could be? ....

b) What is the smallest whole number it could be? ....

ROMAN NUMERALS

These are the Roman numerals:

I is 1   V is 5   X is 10   L is 50   C is 100   D is 500   M is 1,000

Rosa breaks away a block from the floor, glad that she chopped away from where she is standing. Below the terracotta block is a very deep pit. If she had broken the floor anywhere else, she might have fallen in! As she peers in, she can see four chests and some signs. She slowly begins digging down, block by block.

 1

Three of the signs feature Roman numerals. Help Rosa to find the value of them.

a)  LXXVII ....

b)  CIX ....

c)  DCLV ....

2

Draw lines to match the Roman numerals to the correct numbers.

CXLV	CCXX	XCVI	CDIX	CXXII

122	96	145	220	409

As Rosa reaches the bottom of the pit, she notices the floor below her looks strange. Carefully, she breaks away the tile to find it isn't a slab or a building block. It's a pressure plate...connected to TNT! Was this a trick all along? Rosa harvests the TNT and begins to look through the chests.

3

Inside the chests are emeralds, diamonds and saddles for horses. There is also a mysterious book, which has more Roman numerals shown inside.

Can you decode the numerals for Rosa?

MMXIV

....

4

Look at these seven Roman numerals:

L	C	I	X	D	X	I

a)   Use any four letters once only to make the largest number.   ....

b)   Use any four letters once only to make the smallest number.   ....

c)   Use any of the letters once only to make the number closest to CCL.   ....

5

Solve these calculations and write your answers in Roman numerals.

a)   LX + L = ...

b)   CXCVI ÷ 2 = ...

c)   DCVII + CCII = ...

d)   M ÷ IV = ...

e)   XXX × IX = ...

COLOUR IN HOW MANY EMERALDS YOU EARNED

NEGATIVE NUMBERS

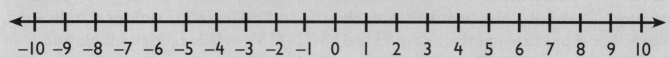

Negative numbers can be shown on a number line:

$$-10\ -9\ -8\ -7\ -6\ -5\ -4\ -3\ -2\ -1\ \ 0\ \ 1\ \ 2\ \ 3\ \ 4\ \ 5\ \ 6\ \ 7\ \ 8\ \ 9\ \ 10$$

Counting on 3 from −1 gives the answer 2.

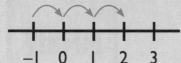

$$-1\ \ 0\ \ 1\ \ 2\ \ 3$$

Counting back 4 from −5 gives the answer −9.

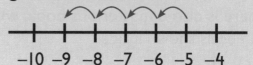

$$-10\ -9\ -8\ -7\ -6\ -5\ -4$$

Rosa is sure this was all a trick from the start. Instead of building back up from inside the pit, she begins to dig sideways, so that she can pop up out of the ground away from the pyramid. It's a lot colder deep underground. Rosa digs faster to get back to the warmth.

1

Circle the warmest temperature in each set.

a)   3°C   −5°C   0°C

b)   −2°C   0°C   −1°C

c)   −7°C   −3°C   −10°C

2

Work out the number that is:

a)   5 greater than −3   ....

b)   3 less than −5   ....

3

Which number comes next in each sequence?

a)   27   21   15   9   3   ....

b)   13   10   7   4   1   ....

Rosa is not sure how far underground she has gone. She knows that digging straight up is dangerous, especially in the desert, as sand can fall and cut off the air supply. To be safe, she digs up one layer at a time, creating a type of stairway. It is a long way up to the surface, so help Rosa dig her way out by tackling these number problems.

4

This diagram shows all the layers that Rosa is digging through:

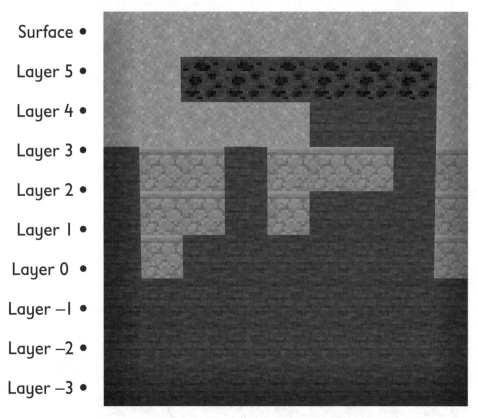

Surface •

Layer 5 •

Layer 4 •

Layer 3 •

Layer 2 •

Layer 1 •

Layer 0 •

Layer −1 •

Layer −2 •

Layer −3 •

Rosa starts at layer 0. From there, she goes down three layers. Then she goes up seven layers to find a chunk of coal ore.

On which layer is the coal ore? ....

5

Look at these temperatures in different biomes.

Biome	Snowy tundra	Mountains	Plains	Jungle	Desert
Temperature	−4°C	−1°C	15°C	25°C	35°C

How many degrees colder is it in the snowy tundra than in the mountains? ....°C

PROPERTIES OF NUMBERS

When two whole numbers are multiplied, the answer is a *multiple*: 4 × 5 = 20 (20 is a multiple of 4 and 5).

A *factor* is a number that is multiplied to get another number: 4 × 5 = 20 (4 and 5 are factors of 20). 4 and 5 are a *factor pair* of 20.

A *prime number* is a number greater than 1 that can only be made by multiplying itself and 1. An example of a prime number is 5.

A *square number* is the result of multiplying a number by itself. $3^2 = 3 \times 3 = 9$

A *cube number* is the result of multiplying a number by itself twice. $3^3 = 3 \times 3 \times 3 = 27$

Once Rosa breaks out of the surface, she dashes off to where the desert meets the jungle. Deciding she likes the look of this area, Rosa builds a small base to rest and sort through what she found.

 1

Rosa starts by harvesting some melon to restore her health. She cuts 24 slices. List all the factor pairs of 24.

2

Next, Rosa sorts the loot from the desert pyramid. Circle all the prime numbers you can see in her quantities of items.

2   9   11   14   17   20

Rosa found some helpful and interesting items in the desert pyramid. She has iron ingots to make a new sword and pickaxe, with some left over. She's not sure how she will use the **TNT**, but she will happily spend the emeralds as soon as she sees a trader.

3

a) $5^2 =$ ....

b) $2^3 =$ ....

c) $10^2 =$ ....

4

Write any common factor of 24 and 63, except for 1.   ....

5

Find the lowest common multiple of:

a)   4 and 6   ....

b)   8 and 12   ....

c)   6 and 9   ....

d)   4 and 7   ....

6

List all the prime numbers between 80 and 90.

....

7

   Which two square numbers total 100?

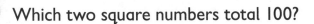 10 and 10

WORD PROBLEMS

Rosa likes this area of jungle and desert so much that she decides to stay for a while. While she takes a break, practise some of the skills you have been learning on this adventure.

1

There are **184,820** blocks between Rosa's new shelter and her home.

How many blocks are there to the nearest hundred thousand? ....

2

The temperature in the mountains one night is −3°C.

The temperature in the desert at night is 10°C.

What is the difference in degrees between the two temperatures? ....°C

3

While building, Rosa finds an old sign with these Roman numerals displayed on it:

MCMXII

What year does the sign show? ....

4

❤ Which two different square numbers less than 20 add together to make another square number?

.... and ....

COLOUR IN HOW MANY EMERALDS YOU EARNED

ADVENTURE ROUND-UP

A MOMENT OF PEACE

Rosa sits in peace in her new base. She already has a large house out on the plains but decides that this will be a perfect place to stay while exploring this area. The noises of the jungle come from one side, while the gentle sounds of the sand flows come from the other. As Rosa flicks through the pages of the book she found, and chomps on a melon slice, a bright blue parrot lands outside her window.

PET PARROT

Fetching some wheat seeds from tufts of jungle grass, Rosa feeds the parrot. After pecking the seeds from her hand, it seems the bird quite likes her and it flies up onto her shoulder. Not only has Rosa found treasure and a peaceful spot to stay, but she also has a new friend. What would you call a pet parrot?

JOBS BEFORE THE MOBS

Rosa eventually gets busy. She smelts sand into glass and harvests cocoa beans for baking. Then she enjoys the quiet... that is before the mobs come out at night!

ADDITION, SUBTRACTION, MULTIPLICATION AND DIVISION

SUNNY SAVANNA

In the savanna, acacia trees can be found sprouting up between tall grass which covers most of the land. There's a lot of flat ground, which makes it a suitable location to build a house or to set up a temporary base for an adventure. The savanna grass is slightly faded, due to the hot sun beating down.

FRIENDS AND ENEMIES

Occasional villages can be seen under construction from the orange acacia wood. These bright and colourful hubs are full of the usual villagers ready to trade or welcome a weary traveller. At night, the savanna is as dangerous as many other biomes.

A COMPANION OF SORTS

All kinds of four-legged animals live in the savanna, including sheep and donkeys. Horses trudge among the tall grass alongside llamas. An adventurer who finds a saddle can have their pick of companions to carry them off to other places.

BIG IDEAS

Isaac has set up camp in the savanna, where he enjoys meeting new people, building interesting things and trading with the local villagers. Isaac now has some big plans...

ADDITION AND SUBTRACTION

Isaac's storage room is well-stocked with materials from expeditions in other biomes. His plan is to use these to start constructing a city in the savanna – a place for fellow adventurers to relax and replenish their resources. Before Isaac starts building, he calculates the quantities of blocks he might need.

1

a) 60,200 + 800 = _6 1,000_ acacia planks

b) 70,000 – 900 = _____ oak planks

c) 55,100 + 55,200 = _____ cobblestone

d) 78,650 – 77,645 = _____ clay

2

Find the missing numbers:

a) 82,738 + _____ = 128,710

b) 92,622 – _____ = 51,512

3

Complete these calculations.

a)
```
  3 4 7
  4 6 8 1
-   1 9 7 9
  _____
    2 7 0 2
```

b)
```
    4 6 2 7
+   5 3 8 7
  _____
```

c)
```
    8 5 4 3
-   6 4 5 1
  _____
```

d)
```
    2 3 5 4
+   7 0 1 9
  _____
```

Isaac has a lot of building blocks ready for his ambitious project, but he will need many more. He expects lots of visitors to stop and rest in the city so he plans to build a large housing area using wooden planks. He will need a lot of wood! Before leaving camp to chop down trees, Isaac enchants his diamond axe with Efficiency. This will speed up the task.

4

Look at this sum: 5,933 + 3,473 + 14,491

Estimate the answer to this sum by rounding each number to the nearest thousand.

....

5

Calculate:

a) 495,539 − 382,578

....

b) 254,636 + 431,508

....

6

Find the missing numbers in these calculations.

a)
```
      6 [ ] 8 9
  +   2 5 [ ] 4
  ─────────────
      8 9 7 3
```

b)
```
      7 [ ] 8 3
  −   2 4 7 [ ]
  ─────────────
      4 6 0 4
```

Having collected thousands and thousands of wooden planks, Isaac is ready to build the houses in what will be the central area of the city. Wood is a very basic material but can be used in so many crafting recipes, including beds, chests and doors. It's a good job Isaac has so much!

7

Round the numbers to the nearest ten thousand and give the estimated answer.

a) 68,651 – 23,425 ....

b) 76,234 + 45,098 ....

c) 94,343 – 66,720 ....

d) 14,495 + 15,502 ....

8

One of Isaac's structures will require 10,388 wooden planks.

He fits 6,178 wooden planks in week 1.

He adds another 1,894 wooden planks in week 2.

How many more wooden planks does he need to install to complete the structure?

.... wooden planks

COLOUR IN HOW MANY EMERALDS YOU EARNED

ADDITION AND SUBTRACTION WORD PROBLEMS

Once the housing area is finished, Isaac turns his attention to entertainment facilities. Using blocks of lighter shades, he builds a stadium where adventurers can gather to play games like spleef.

1

Isaac's friends, Jacob, Cali, Oscar and Maya, play five games of spleef. Isaac awards them points depending on how well they do in each game.

Player	Game 1	Game 2	Game 3	Game 4	Game 5
Jacob	23,493	10,293	22,371	9,394	42,092
Cali	18,273	21,384	54,109	23,384	55,092
Oscar	10,273	53,235	33,482	18,492	56,099
Maya	29,302	47,038	39,272	8,094	9,102

a) Which player scored the most points? ....

b) How many more points in total did Maya get than Jacob? ....

2

Isaac's sports stadium has 20,569 seats.

3,029 of these seats are reserved for special guests.

How many seats are **not** reserved for special guests? .... seats

While lots of adventurers want to rest or play games together, others like to relax with a good book. Isaac begins work on a vast library. Adventurers can borrow books to take away or read in quiet, cosy corners. Isaac has also created an enchantment area, where people can come and place new enchantments on their tools and weapons.

3

On the opening day, the downstairs floor of Isaac's library had 5,245 books available to borrow.

There were 2,789 more books available on the shelves of the upstairs floor.

During the first month:

- Isaac crafted 750 more books and made them available to borrow
- borrowers took away 2,144 books to read
- 378 books had to be destroyed because they got damaged.

How many books were available to borrow at the end of the month? .... books

4

Isaac starts with 125,000 paper to craft even more books.

He loses thirty thousand paper.

Then he loses another 8,000 paper.

How much paper does he have left? .... paper

5

A library in a neighbouring biome has capacity for 22,000 books. There are four floors in this library.

Three of the floors can hold 3,835, 4,087 and 7,266 books.

How many books can the fourth floor hold? .... books

 COLOUR IN HOW MANY EMERALDS YOU EARNED

MULTIPLICATION

Some of Isaac's friends keep bringing him new materials and items to use while developing the city. They've kindly been placing them in some chests in his camp, but it has become rather untidy. Help Isaac count up these items so he can organise them properly.

1

Work out:

a) 37 × 100 = ... sugar cane

b) 946 × 10 = ... paper

c) 23 × 1,000 = ... leather

d) 30 × 20 = ... glass bottles

e) 12 × 500 = ... Nether wart

f) 40 × 900 = ... gunpowder

2

Work out the answers to some more calculations.

a) 32 × 27 = ...

b) 119 × 12 = ...

c) 275 × 43 = ...

d) 7,326 × 15 = ...

Isaac keeps building, and the size of the city continues to multiply at a rate of thousands of blocks per day.

3

Make the scales balance by writing the correct value on the other side.

a)

30×12^2

b)

12×5^3

4

Find the missing numbers in these calculations.

a)

$$
\begin{array}{r}
6\ \square\ 7\ \square \\
\times \qquad 4 \\
\hline
2\ 6\ 3\ 1\ 2 \\
\hline
\end{array}
$$

b)

$$
\begin{array}{r}
\square\ 4\ \square\ 7 \\
\times \qquad 6 \\
\hline
1\ 4\ 9\ 2\ 2 \\
\hline
\end{array}
$$

5

Use each of the digits 5, 6, 7, 8 and the × sign once to make:

a)   the multiplication calculation with
     the largest possible answer.   ....

b)   the multiplication calculation with
     the smallest possible answer.   ....

DIVISION

Next on Isaac's list is a working farm, from where visitors can take some supplies after helping to plant and tend crops. The huge quantities of food produced will also be divided among the city's needy residents.

1

Work out these crop calculations.

a)   156,000 potatoes ÷ 10 = ... potatoes

b)   14,000 carrots ÷ 2,000 = ... carrots

c)   54,000 beetroot ÷ 900 = ... beetroot

2

Now work out these food calculations.

a)   744 pumpkin pie ÷ 3 = ... pumpkin pie

b)   525 cookies ÷ 5 = ... cookies

c)   392 cocoa beans ÷ 7 = ... cocoa beans

d)   6,844 eggs ÷ 4 = ... eggs

e)   5,064 wheat ÷ 8 = ... wheat

f)   6,174 sugar ÷ 9 = ... sugar

The city is now open to all visitors. After some time, Isaac notices that many heroes are asking for a place to store their emeralds, so they don't get lost. Isaac announces that he will build a bank, where everyone can store their valuables safely. In the vault, Isaac places traps and heavy iron doors for extra security. The vault is already filling up fast!

3

Find the missing numbers.

a) .... emeralds × 6 = 7,488 emeralds

b) .... emeralds × 7 = 6,888 emeralds

4

Write the missing numbers in these short division calculations.

a)

$$4 \overline{) 2\,\square\,4\,\square} = 5\,6\,2 \text{ r } 2$$

b)

$$6 \overline{) 5\,\square\,7\,\square} = 8\,7\,9$$

5

A wealthy visitor brings 543 diamonds to store safely in the bank. The diamonds are stored in small stacks.

Each small stack holds 6 diamonds.

How many diamonds are left over?

.... diamonds

MULTIPLICATION AND DIVISION WORD PROBLEMS

Isaac is happy with how his city turned out. But he has forgotten one very important thing...where will he live? All this time he has stayed in his small camp! Isaac chooses one of the shops in the city and builds an extra floor on top. This is where he will live, while downstairs he will sell clothes and armour. Using leather from his storage, he begins crafting leggings to sell.

1

Isaac makes leggings from leather.

He has 3 chests containing 750 leather each.

He uses 7 leather for each set of leggings.

How many full sets of leggings can Isaac make?

.... leggings

2

Isaac is thinking of a secret number.

He multiplies his secret number by 7.

Then he divides the result by 8.

The answer is 1,176.

What is Isaac's secret number? ....

3

 Isaac has made 53 iron helmets. He places them in stacks of 4 and 5 inside a chest.

How many stacks contain 4 helmets, and how many stacks contain 5 helmets? Give one possible answer.

....

COLOUR IN HOW MANY EMERALDS YOU EARNED

ADVENTURE ROUND-UP

SAVANNA SUCCESS

Isaac has established a successful and thriving city in the savanna, calculating some very big numbers along the way!

A NICE CHANGE

While building, crafting and selling, Isaac has learned lots of new skills. It has made a change from exploring dangerous biomes and fighting mobs.

STORYTIME

As the sun begins to set behind the tall buildings of the city, Isaac treats himself to a slice of cake and a few pages of his favourite book. This one is all about life in the swamps and it sparks his interest in that biome.

FRACTIONS (INCLUDING DECIMALS)

THE SCENE IN THE SNOWY TUNDRA

In the snowy tundra, very little breaks through the thick snow which covers the ground. Aside from tall spruce trees and the odd poppy, the snow is unbroken. The river surface is frozen and can be walked across. As the snowy tundra extends out into the sea, ice spikes reach out of the deep waters. These conditions make it slippery underfoot but the ice can be harvested with the right tools.

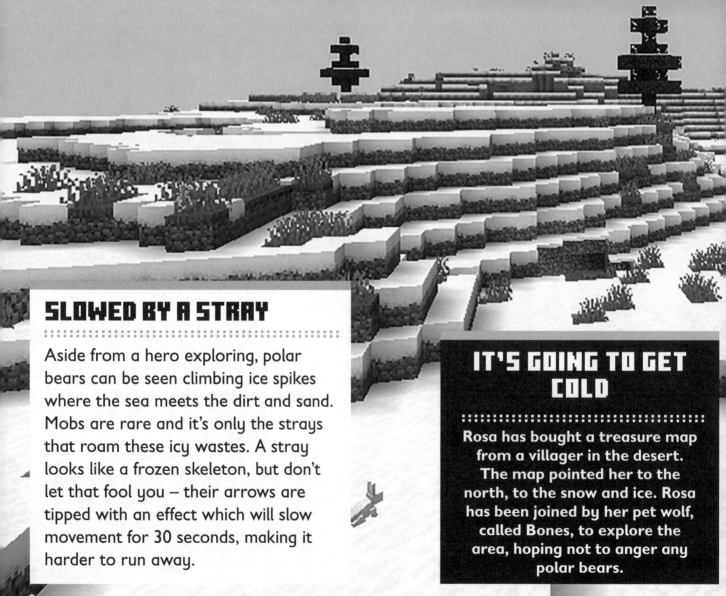

SLOWED BY A STRAY

Aside from a hero exploring, polar bears can be seen climbing ice spikes where the sea meets the dirt and sand. Mobs are rare and it's only the strays that roam these icy wastes. A stray looks like a frozen skeleton, but don't let that fool you – their arrows are tipped with an effect which will slow movement for 30 seconds, making it harder to run away.

IT'S GOING TO GET COLD

Rosa has bought a treasure map from a villager in the desert. The map pointed her to the north, to the snow and ice. Rosa has been joined by her pet wolf, called Bones, to explore the area, hoping not to anger any polar bears.

EQUIVALENT FRACTIONS

Warm up for Rosa's adventure through the snowy tundra by studying this fractions wall.

I whole											
$\frac{1}{2}$						$\frac{1}{2}$					
$\frac{1}{3}$				$\frac{1}{3}$				$\frac{1}{3}$			
$\frac{1}{4}$			$\frac{1}{4}$			$\frac{1}{4}$			$\frac{1}{4}$		
$\frac{1}{6}$		$\frac{1}{6}$		$\frac{1}{6}$		$\frac{1}{6}$		$\frac{1}{6}$		$\frac{1}{6}$	
$\frac{1}{12}$	$\frac{1}{12}$	$\frac{1}{12}$	$\frac{1}{12}$	$\frac{1}{12}$	$\frac{1}{12}$	$\frac{1}{12}$	$\frac{1}{12}$	$\frac{1}{12}$	$\frac{1}{12}$	$\frac{1}{12}$	$\frac{1}{12}$

 1

Complete the missing numbers in these equivalent fractions.

a) $\frac{1}{3} = \frac{\square}{6}$

b) $\frac{3}{4} = \frac{9}{\square}$

c) $\frac{10}{12} = \frac{\square}{6}$

2

Complete the missing numbers in these sets of equivalent fractions.

a) $\frac{1}{10} = \frac{2}{\square} = \frac{\square}{30}$

b) $\frac{2}{3} = \frac{4}{\square} = \frac{\square}{12}$

3

Write three fractions equivalent to $\frac{1}{2}$

....

IMPROPER FRACTIONS AND MIXED NUMBERS

$$2 + \frac{3}{4} = \frac{8}{4} + \frac{3}{4} = \frac{11}{4}$$

$$2\frac{3}{4} = \frac{11}{4}$$

A mixed number has a whole number part and a fraction part.

In an improper fraction the numerator is greater than the denominator.

1

Draw lines to match each mixed number to its equivalent improper fraction.

$4\frac{3}{5}$	$\frac{34}{5}$
$8\frac{2}{10}$	$8\frac{2}{9}$
$\frac{7}{3}$	$\frac{82}{10}$
$\frac{8}{4}$	$2\frac{1}{3}$
$6\frac{4}{5}$	$\frac{23}{5}$
$\frac{8}{3}$	2
$\frac{74}{9}$	$2\frac{2}{3}$

Before she gets too far into the snowy tundra, Rosa decides to build two tall columns of cobblestone that she will be able to see from a distance and will help to guide her back. She makes one column but runs out of cobblestone while building the second column. Never mind, $1\frac{1}{2}$ columns is better than none at all!

2

Change these mixed numbers to improper fractions.

a) $2\frac{1}{2} = \dfrac{\square}{2}$

b) $3\frac{2}{5} = \dfrac{\square}{5}$

c) $4\frac{5}{8} = \dfrac{\square}{8}$

3

Change these improper fractions into mixed numbers.

a) $\dfrac{7}{2} = \text{..............}$

b) $\dfrac{11}{3} = \text{..............}$

c) $\dfrac{23}{10} = \text{..............}$

4

Write $\dfrac{37}{12}$ as a mixed number.

....

5

 Write $67\frac{1}{6}$ as an improper fraction.

$\square$

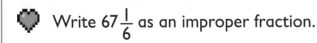

COMPARING AND ORDERING FRACTIONS

Rosa has brought plenty of food for this expedition, but will it be enough? To make sure she doesn't run out of supplies, she keeps track of what fraction of the food items in her inventory is left available.

I

In each pair of fractions below, which is the larger fraction of the whole shape?

Use the diagram to help you. Circle your answers.

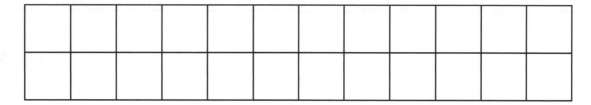

a) $\frac{1}{2}$ or $\frac{4}{6}$

b) $\frac{7}{12}$ or $\frac{10}{24}$

c) $\frac{3}{4}$ or $\frac{7}{8}$

2

In each pair of fractions below, which is the smaller fraction of the whole shape?

Use the diagrams to help you. Circle your answers.

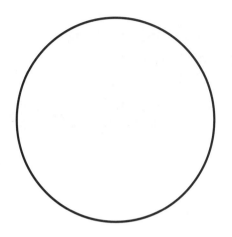 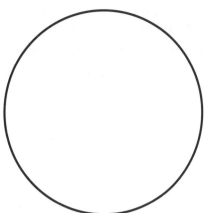 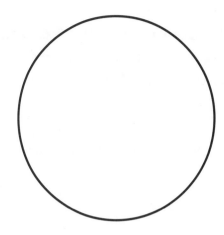

a) $\frac{3}{5}$ or $\frac{4}{10}$

b) $\frac{5}{9}$ or $\frac{1}{3}$

c) $\frac{3}{8}$ or $\frac{1}{2}$

3

Write **<** or **>** in the boxes to make each statement correct.

a) $1\frac{1}{6}$ ☐ $\frac{8}{6}$

b) $2\frac{3}{4}$ ☐ $\frac{9}{4}$

c) $4\frac{1}{3}$ ☐ $\frac{12}{3}$

4

Circle the largest fraction in each pair.

a) $\frac{2}{3}$ $\frac{11}{15}$

b) $\frac{4}{5}$ $\frac{13}{20}$

c) $\frac{1}{4}$ $\frac{5}{12}$

5

Circle the smallest fraction in each set.

a) $\frac{4}{5}$ $\frac{11}{15}$ $\frac{7}{10}$ $\frac{13}{20}$

b) $\frac{5}{6}$ $\frac{7}{9}$ $\frac{11}{12}$ $\frac{2}{3}$

ADDING AND SUBTRACTING FRACTIONS

Treading carefully, Rosa plods through the snow and onto the ice. Slipping a little, she steadies her footing and looks up at the spikes of ice towering above her. She uses fractions to compare the heights of the ice spikes.

1

Answer these fraction calculations.

a) $\dfrac{1}{5} + \dfrac{2}{5} =$ ☐

b) $\dfrac{8}{10} - \dfrac{1}{10} =$ ☐

c) $1 - \dfrac{2}{3} =$ ☐

d) $\dfrac{1}{2} + \dfrac{1}{4} =$ ☐

e) $\dfrac{1}{5} + \dfrac{1}{10} =$ ☐

f) $\dfrac{1}{2} - \dfrac{1}{6} =$ ☐

2

Write the answer to each calculation as an improper fraction.

a) $\dfrac{5}{8} + \dfrac{7}{8} =$ ☐

b) $\dfrac{18}{7} - \dfrac{6}{7} =$ ☐

c) $\dfrac{2}{3} + \dfrac{1}{3} + \dfrac{2}{3} =$ ☐

d) $\dfrac{1}{2} + \dfrac{1}{4} + \dfrac{1}{2} =$ ☐

Not too far away, Rosa spots a polar bear and her cub walking across the shards of ice. Rosa knows that if she approaches them, even carefully, the mother bear will become angry. She will defend her cub. Rosa drops cod and salmon on the ice in various amounts, hoping they will find it.

3

Write the answer to each calculation as a mixed number.

a) $\frac{3}{5} + \frac{4}{5} =$ ....

b) $\frac{10}{12} + \frac{5}{12} =$ ....

c) $\frac{3}{7} + \frac{9}{7} =$ ....

d) $\frac{16}{3} + \frac{7}{3} =$ ....

4

The mother polar bear eats $\frac{3}{12}$ of a stack of fish.

The baby bear eats $\frac{4}{12}$ of the same stack of fish.

What fraction of the stack of fish is left?

5

 Find the missing numbers in these fraction calculations.

a) $\frac{11}{12} + \frac{\Box}{12} = 1\frac{7}{12}$

b) $\frac{\Box}{3} + \frac{1}{6} = 1\frac{5}{6}$

c) $\frac{7}{8} + \frac{3}{\Box} = 1\frac{5}{8}$

COLOUR IN HOW MANY EMERALDS YOU EARNED

ORDERING AND ROUNDING DECIMALS

Rosa has already collected some snow because she wants to build a snow golem, which will help to protect her home. She would like to take some ice with her, too. In order to harvest the ice without it breaking up, Rosa must use her pickaxe enchanted with Silk Touch.

1

These decimals show how long in seconds it takes Rosa to harvest some of the ice blocks.

Write the decimals in order, smallest first.

a)   6.452   6.542   6.245   6.254

....

b)   11.1   11.18   11.081   11.018

....

2

Round each decimal to the nearest whole number.

a)   6.49   ....   b)   11.91   ....

c)   219.37   ....   d)   5,726.82   ....

3

While Rosa works, her pet wolf Bones runs across the ice sheet four times. Here are the times Bones achieves on each run.

Run 1: 14.149 seconds   **Run 2:** 14.492 seconds

Run 3: 14.942 seconds   **Run 4:** 14.194 seconds

Which run was the fastest? ....

4

Here are some more times in seconds. Round each number to 1 decimal place.

a)   7.07   ....

b)   25.61   ....

c)   3.96   ....

d)   752.15   ....

e)   2,450.73   ....

f)   50,106.85   ....

5

Which number is the odd one out? Use rounding to explain.

8.43

9.11

8.57

9.36

8.94

Answer: ....

Explanation: ....

....

FRACTION AND DECIMAL EQUIVALENTS

Remember how many digits come after the decimal point when converting fractions with a denominator of 10, 100 or 1,000 into decimals:

$\frac{3}{10} = 0.3$ $\frac{9}{100} = 0.09$ $\frac{81}{100} = 0.81$ $\frac{507}{1,000} = 0.507$

As Rosa walks on, she spots an odd lump in the snow in the distance. When she gets closer, she sees a door in the snow. It's an igloo! On entering, she realises it's been abandoned: books and glass bottles are left discarded and there are no signs of life. Rosa breaks away the carpet to take home when she finds a ladder. She climbs down and finds a potion workshop.

1

Write the decimal equivalent for each fraction of the ladder that Rosa climbs down.

a)   One quarter = ...   b)   One fifth = ...

c)   One half = ...   d)   Two fifths = ...

e)   Four tenths = ...   f)   Seven hundredths = ...

2

Rosa puts $\frac{3}{4}$ of a kilogram of glowstone dust on a set of digital scales.

What is the decimal reading on the scales?   .... kg

Inside the workshop Rosa finds another chest, which contains a golden apple. There is also a brewing stand with a completed splash Potion of Weakness. What a strange collection of items! Suddenly a groaning sound echoes through the basement. Rosa turns slowly, worried about what she might find. A zombie's arms are reaching out towards her through a set of iron bars!

3

Write these fractions as decimals.

a) $\dfrac{8}{100}$ = ...

b) $\dfrac{9}{10}$ = ...

c) $\dfrac{29}{100}$ = ...

d) $\dfrac{439}{1,000}$ = ...

e) $\dfrac{51}{1,000}$ = ...

f) $\dfrac{3}{1,000}$ = ...

4

Write each decimal as a fraction.

a) 0.7 =

b) 0.03 =

c) 0.607 =

d) 0.501 =

e) 0.097 =

f) 0.777 =

5

Write a decimal number to make each statement correct.

a) .... < 3 tenths

b) .... < $\dfrac{3}{4}$

c) $\dfrac{3}{20}$ < ....

d) $\dfrac{7}{25}$ > ....

COLOUR IN HOW MANY EMERALDS YOU EARNED

FRACTION, DECIMAL AND PERCENTAGE EQUIVALENTS

'per cent' means 'out of 100'.

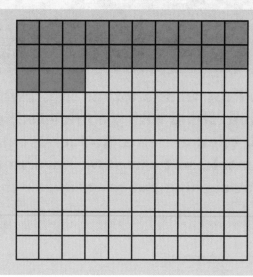

$23\% = \dfrac{23}{100} = 0.23$

Rosa looks again at the golden apple and the splash Potion of Weakness. Perhaps the person who used to live here was trying to cure the zombie. It looks like the zombie was once a villager. Rosa wonders how long they have been stuck down here and wants to try to cure them.

1

Write each percentage as a fraction.

a) 5% =

b) 29% =

c) 43% =

d) 87% =

2

Write each percentage as a decimal.

a) 9% = ...

b) 50% = ...

c) 67% = ...

d) 99% = ...

3

Write these decimals and fractions as percentages.

a) 0.57 = ...%

b) 0.3 = ...%

c) 0.01 = ...%

d) $\dfrac{13}{100}$ = ...%

e) $\dfrac{1}{4}$ = ...%

f) $\dfrac{9}{10}$ = ...%

Rosa is a bit scared being this close to a zombie villager. She then closes her eyes tightly and throws the splash Potion of Weakness at the zombie. Quickly, she gives them the golden apple and backs away. Will this even work?

4

Find **eight** pairs of equivalent fractions, decimals or percentages.

Use different coloured pencils to join the pairs.

100%

0.2

$\frac{3}{50}$

20%

$\frac{3}{10}$

85%

60%

0.01

$\frac{10}{10}$

$\frac{85}{100}$

6%

30%

1%

0.6

0.4

$\frac{2}{5}$

5

 Rosa must coat 80% of the zombie with the potion.

The zombie is divided into 20 equal sections.

How many sections must she coat with the potion? ....

COLOUR IN HOW MANY EMERALDS YOU EARNED

41

MULTIPLYING FRACTIONS

With the apple eaten, the zombie's skin loses its green colour, and their arms drop to the side of their body. Rosa waves her hand in front of their eyes. Fraction by fraction, the zombie changes back into their original self. It's an amazing experience for both of them! They both climb the ladder and leave the igloo.

1

$\frac{2}{3}$ of each bar is shaded:

Work out the answers to each calculation as an improper fraction and as a mixed or whole number.

a) $\frac{2}{3} \times 2 = $ ⬜ = ...

b) $4 \times \frac{2}{3} = $ ⬜ = ...

c) $\frac{2}{3} \times 3 = $ ⬜ = ...

2

$\frac{3}{5}$ of this bar is shaded:

Work out the answers to each calculation as an improper fraction and a mixed number.

a) $\frac{3}{5} \times 3 = $ ⬜ = ...

b) $\frac{2}{5} \times 4 = $ ⬜ = ...

3

Work out the answer to each calculation as a fraction or a whole number. Use this grid to help if you wish.

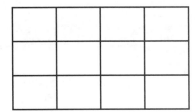

a) $\dfrac{1}{12} \times 6 =$ ☐

b) $5 \times \dfrac{1}{4} =$ ☐

c) $\dfrac{3}{4} \times 3 =$ ☐

d) $8 \times \dfrac{1}{4} =$ ☐

4

Work out these. Give your answers as fractions or whole numbers.

a) $6 \times \dfrac{1}{2} =$ ☐

b) $3 \times \dfrac{1}{6} =$ ☐

c) $3 \times \dfrac{5}{12} =$ ☐

5

 Write your answers to these calculations as mixed numbers. Use the diagram below to help you.

  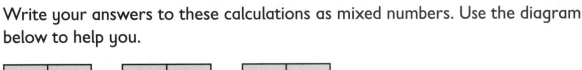

a) $2\dfrac{3}{4} \times 2 =$ ....

b) $3 \times 2\dfrac{3}{4} =$ ....

c) $1\dfrac{3}{4} \times 5 =$ ....

WORD PROBLEMS

Rosa and the villager look out across the snow. She will walk them back to their home in the mountains.

1

Rosa, Bones and the villager have completed 60% of their journey to the mountains.

What percentage of the journey is left? ....%

2

Rosa has food on her mind. A recipe for cakes uses $\frac{3}{4}$ of a litre of milk to make 5 cakes.

How many litres of milk do you need to make 30 cakes? .... litres

---

3

A village baker in the mountains sells three types of sweet food.

$\frac{3}{8}$ of the food is cookies.

$\frac{1}{4}$ of the food is pumpkin pie.

The rest of the food is cake.

What fraction of the food is cake?

ADVENTURE ROUND-UP

ZOMBIE SURPRISE

Rosa's trip through the snow and ice threw up some surprises. She certainly did not expect to cure a zombie and escort them home!

SNOW SECURED

Rosa is really looking forward to getting home and trying out new potions, as well as building her snow golem with the blocks of snow she harvested. Before she does any of that, Rosa thinks a trip through the local mountains would be a nice detour on her journey home. With the villager safely back at home, Rosa sets off with Bones.

MEASUREMENT

MURKY AND MUDDY

The swamps are a gloomy and drab place in the Overworld. The grass is a muddy green and vines creep up the trunks of the oak trees. The lakes are shallow and lily pads float on the surface, but there are no fish in the murky waters. Pockets of clay form where the water meets the dirt and can be dug out and baked into bricks.

SLIMY THREAT

At the edges of the lakes, plenty of sugar cane grows. Mushrooms dot the landscape and occasionally huge mushrooms sprout up tall enough to walk underneath. There are plenty of mobs and friendly animals shuffling around. Swamps are one of the places where slimes can spawn, especially during a full moon.

WITCH OUT!

If an adventurer is unlucky, they may stumble across a swamp hut, where a witch lives with their black cat. The witch is a nasty mob that throws harmful potions around, hoping to hurt anyone who enters the swamp. The witch's hut will often have a cauldron that can be used to hold water for potion brewing.

SAMPLING THE SWAMPS

Having established a city in the savanna, Isaac is now looking for some peace and quiet and the chance to brew some potions. Reading about the swamps prompted him to come here. He has built a small, temporary home and will establish a farm to make sure he has a good supply of food while he's here.

UNITS OF MEASURE

Length	Mass	Capacity
1 cm = 10 mm	1 kg = 1,000 g	1 l = 1,000 ml
1 m = 100 cm	1 t = 1,000 kg	
1 km = 1,000 m		

- 1 inch is about 2.5 cm
- 1 pound is about 450 g
- 1 pint is about 550 ml

Isaac starts off by measuring out space to grow crops. He must measure the space in blocks. Isaac wants to lay blocks of dirt into the shallow pools to create rows for planting vegetables.

Convert these to check your understanding of metric measures.

a) 6 kg = ... g

b) 4,000 ml = ... l

c) 3 t = ... kg

d) 7 km = ... m

e) $\frac{1}{2}$ m = ... cm

f) 5 cm = ... mm

Three of the vegetable plots are each 4,000 mm long.

Two other vegetable plots are each 2,500 mm long.

What is the total length of these five vegetable plots in metres? .... m

Isaac lays rows of dirt into the water. Being surrounded by water will help the crops to grow quickly and healthily. Using a hoe, he prepares the ground for potatoes, carrots and beetroot. He has planned a second area for wheat.

3

Tick the heaviest chest of potatoes.

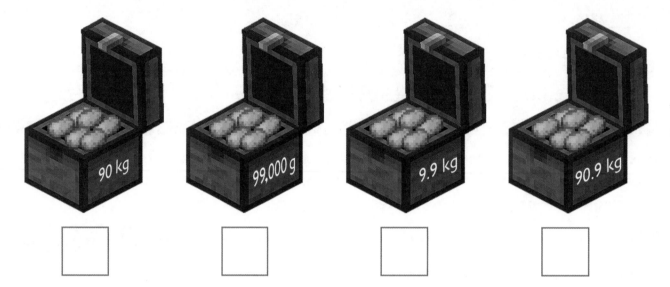

90 kg   99,000 g   9.9 kg   90.9 kg

☐   ☐   ☐   ☐

4

Isaac grows these vegetables: 0.75 kg of beetroot, 0.3 kg of carrots and 2,500 g of potatoes.

a) What is the total mass of the vegetables in kilograms? .... kg

b) Including wheat, the total mass of the crops he grows is 6.15 kg.

What is the mass of the wheat that Isaac grows? .... kg

5

Write **<** or **>** in the boxes to make these statements correct.

a) 0.4 l ☐ 394 ml   b) 6.3 km ☐ 630 m

c) 1,090 mm ☐ 192 cm   d) 505 g ☐ 0.55 kg

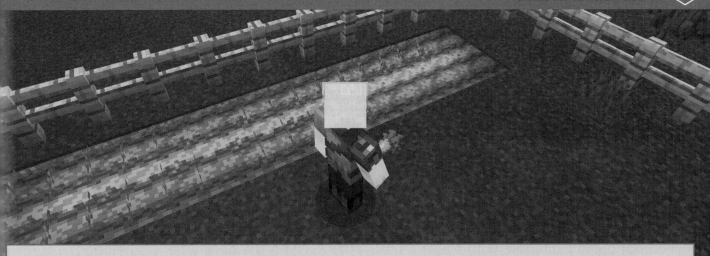

Isaac still has plenty of space for more crops. He would love to brew some potions for his adventure and there's one particular plant he will need for this – Nether wart. This doesn't grow in dirt though; it grows in soul sand. Luckily, he has several blocks to hand, plus a few handfuls of Nether wart.

6

Find the approximate measures.

a) 5 inches is about .... centimetres.

b) 2 pints is about .... litres.

c) 3 pounds is about .... grams.

7

Write **<** or **>** in the boxes to make these statements correct.

a) I litre ☐ I pint   b) 6 inches ☐ 10 cm

c) 300 mm ☐ 8 inches   d) I pound ☐ I kg

8

A container can hold 11 gallons of milk.

I gallon = 8 pints

Approximately how much milk
can the container hold in litres?

.... l

**COLOUR IN HOW MANY
EMERALDS YOU EARNED**

PERIMETER

Now Isaac has planted the vegetables and wheat, he moves on to sugar cane. Sugar cane is important for food recipes but also for crafting books, as it can be made into paper. Isaac plants the sugar cane near a pond.

1

The pond is a rectangle with these measurements. Find the perimeter of the pond.

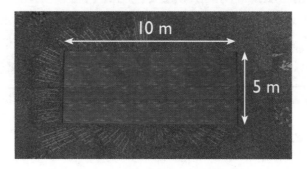

.... m

2

Here is a plan of a square swamp that lies close to Isaac's house.

Find the perimeter of the swamp.

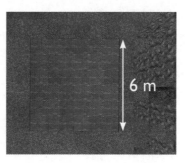

.... m

3

This is a plan of Isaac's sugar cane crop.

Work out the perimeter of the crop.

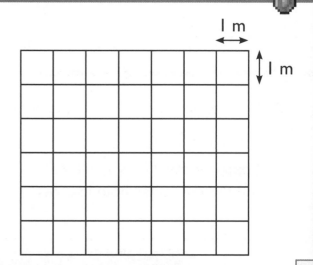

.... m

Isaac has everything he needs to brew potions and build a library for enchanting tools. Now it's time to build the room which will house his brewing stand and enchantment table. To help inspire his potion-brewing, he will decorate the rooms with item frames containing souvenirs from past adventures – a **Wither** skull, his first diamond and his enchanted sword.

4

Find the perimeter of each of these rooms in the potion-brewing building.

a)

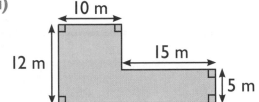

.... m

b)

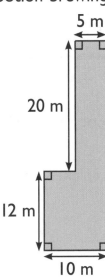

.... m

5

Work out the missing side lengths of these miniature frames.

a)

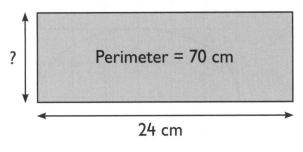

Perimeter = 70 cm

24 cm

.... cm

b)

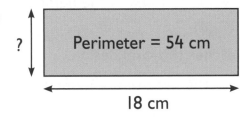

Perimeter = 54 cm

18 cm

.... cm

COLOUR IN HOW MANY EMERALDS YOU EARNED

AREA

Isaac is enjoying this project in the swamp. Next he begins to think about building facilities for keeping animals.

1

Isaac builds a cow shed.

The diagram shows the measurements of the cow shed.

Calculate the area occupied by the cow shed.

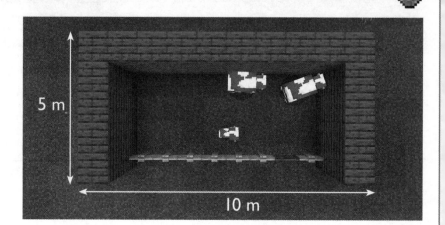

5 m

10 m

.... m²

2

Isaac builds a chicken coop.

From above, the chicken coop is the shape of a square with side length 9 m.

Calculate the area of the chicken coop.

.... m²

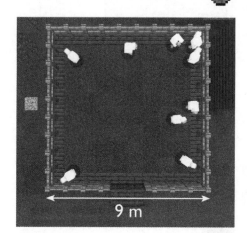

9 m

3

Isaac wants to make some name tags for the animals.

He sketches this oval design.

Estimate the area of the name tag in this design.

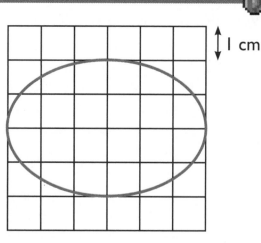

1 cm

.... cm²

The farm is gradually taking shape but Isaac would like to add some small features, including miniature signs and decorations, to make it look as nice and organised as possible. Help him with some more calculations in centimetres.

 4

Find the side length of a square with an area of 64 cm².

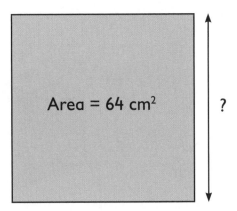

Area = 64 cm²

?

.... cm

5

 Find the perimeter and the area of this shape.

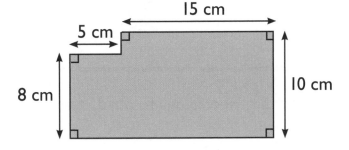

15 cm

5 cm

8 cm

10 cm

Perimeter: .... cm

Area: .... cm²

VOLUME

Isaac would like to add an ornamental touch to his farm so he starts to imagine ways of combining blocks to make different sculptures and other artistic features.

These are models of some of Isaac's creative ideas.

They are made from 1 cm³ cubes.

Find the volume of each model.

a)

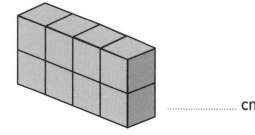

.... cm³

b)

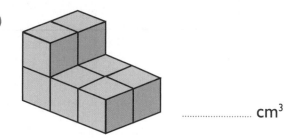

.... cm³

c)

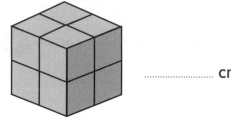

.... cm³

d)

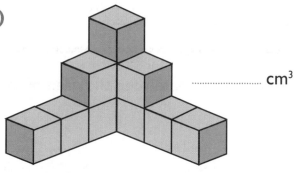

.... cm³

2

Here is a model of a sculpture that Isaac plans to build. It will be a sculpture of a slime.

Find the volume of this model.

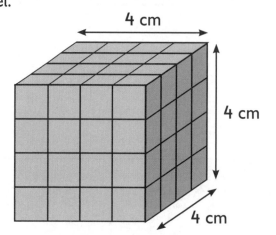

4 cm

4 cm

4 cm

.... cm³

Isaac will need a storage building for farm supplies and produce.

3

Here is a model of a storage building.

The building is cuboid-shaped.

Work out the volume of this model.

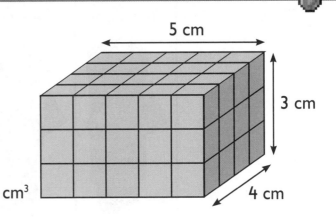

5 cm

3 cm

4 cm

.... cm³

4

Here is another model of a cuboid-shaped building.

It has a 1 cm³ cube in one corner.

Estimate the volume of this model.

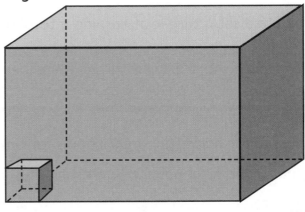

.... cm³

5

 Work out the side length of a cube that has a volume of 27 cm³.

.... cm

MONEY

Isaac needs more emeralds to buy equipment he will need while exploring the swamp. Filling his inventory, he goes to the local village with some food that has already grown and a few other items which he hopes to sell. While Isaac has emeralds on his mind, earn some yourself by answering these questions.

I

The table shows how much money five villagers earned in a day, in pounds and pence.

Villager	Armourer	Shepherd	Butcher	Fletcher	Toolsmith
Money earned	£65.27	£57.76	£49.54	£84.80	£78.42

They had set a target of earning a total of £400 between them.

How much short of their target were they? £ ....

2

The pay for harvesting mushrooms for one hour is £18.75

What is the total pay for harvesting mushrooms for 9 hours? £ ....

3

A chest of mushrooms is on sale for £27.35

A customer buys the mushrooms using two £20 notes.

How much change will be given? £ ....

In the local village, Isaac meets with the farmer. He trades 20 wheat for 1 emerald. They also take some carrots from him. The armourer takes some spare coal for a few more emeralds. Isaac spends his emeralds on arrows and a crossbow to keep mobs at bay.

4

Isaac has the equivalent of two £20 notes, three £5 notes and £6.73 in coins.

In pounds and pence, his arrows and crossbow would cost £28.55

How much money would he have left in pounds and pence?   £ ....

5

 Isaac started last week with £60. He spent 25% of his money.

a) How much money did Isaac spend?   £ ....

b) Rosa only had 50% of the money Isaac started with.
Rosa spent 25% of her money.
How much money did Rosa spend?   £ ....

TIME

Isaac uses his clock to know when the day will turn to night or when to stop for lunch in the middle of the day. The sun will soon set so help him to get home in good time by answering these questions.

 1

A brewing session starts at 10:50 am and lasts for 90 minutes.

At what time does it finish?

....

2

It takes 8 minutes to smelt raw gold into a gold ingot.

How many ingots can be smelted in 8 hours?

.... ingots

 3

What time is 5 hours 12 minutes earlier than 00:32?

....

Isaac arrives home thinking he's safe. Except, as he walks through the gate into his farm, he comes across some slimes bouncing around near the front door. It looks like he'll have to fight to get a peaceful night!

4

A butcher villager started work at 9:45 am.

They worked for 8 hours.

After work, they walked for 5 minutes to the village centre and stayed there for $1\frac{1}{2}$ hours. Then they took 20 minutes to walk home.

At what time did the villager get home? ....

5

Here are the sunrise and sunset times in two different biomes.

How much more daylight did the swamp have than the mountains?

Swamp:	Sunrise at 06:32
	Sunset at 21:33
Mountains:	Sunrise at 06:45
	Sunset at 16:59

.... hours .... minutes

WORD PROBLEMS

Isaac gets up nice and early, ready to explore and bring back some more animals to his farm. He has food ready to attract them – carrots for pigs, wheat for cows and sheep, and some seeds for chickens. While Isaac finds the animals, recap some of the topics covered in the swamp biome.

1

In pounds and pence, it costs £12.80 for four children to visit a farm.

How much does it cost for one child?

£ ....

2

A volunteer works at a farm for 90 minutes three times a week.

How long does the volunteer work at the farm in 5 weeks?

.... hours .... minutes

3

A villager saves 5 emeralds a week.

How many emeralds does the villager save in 1 year?

.... emeralds

Isaac manages to find two of each animal that he wanted. He leads each of them to the farm and they happily explore their barns. By feeding the animals their favourite food, they will have a baby, but Isaac doesn't want them to be crowded. He will release some as they get older.

4

Here is a plan of one of Isaac's barns and adjoining fields.

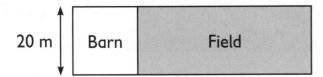

20 m

Barn

Field

The barn and the field are both 20 m wide.

The area of the field is 1,000 m².

How long is the field? .... m

5

Isaac starts feeding the animals at 10:20 am for 1 hour.

It starts to rain $\frac{2}{3}$ of the way through.

At what time does it start to rain? ....

6

A horse leaves its stable at 1:10 pm.

It spends $\frac{1}{4}$ of an hour exploring the farmyard.

It waits 5 minutes to be released into a field and then grazes for 35 minutes.

It takes 5 minutes for the horse to walk back to the stable.

At what time does the horse arrive back at the stable?

....

Isaac has gathered flowers to make the farm more colourful, plus he's crafted fences to keep out the mobs at night. He places blocks of glowstone from the Nether on fence posts to stop hostile mobs spawning nearby. Now put the finishing touches on your measurement skills.

7

A villager makes 7 fence posts that are each 75 cm long.

He cuts the posts from two-metre lengths of wood.

Each two-metre length costs £16.50.

Each fence post is made of only one piece of wood.

How much does the wood for the fence posts cost?

£ ....

8

♥ The length of a rectangular gate is three times its height.

The perimeter of the gate is 960 cm.

Find the length of the gate.

.... cm

COLOUR IN HOW MANY EMERALDS YOU EARNED

ADVENTURE ROUND-UP

SWAMPY SETTLEMENT

Compared to the hustle and bustle of the savanna city, settling down in the swamp has been a welcome change for Isaac. He has been fortunate not to meet a witch, but he can hear them at night, along with slimes bouncing around.

SLIMY PICKINGS

Once Isaac gets more familiar with this biome, he will begin to adventure at night and tackle the mobs. Slimes will drop slimeballs that are very helpful; these can be used to craft leads for animals or sticky pistons, which make great machines.

SHARPENING HIS EYE

For now, Isaac stands on the top floor of his house and practises aiming with his crossbow, firing arrows out into the swamp. He's getting much better and knows this skill will help if he ever wants to face off against the Ender Dragon with Rosa.

GEOMETRY

COLD ON TOP

The mountains can be as desolate as the desert. But while the desert is often very hot, the mountains are cool and become very cold nearer to the peak. As any adventurer climbs the cliffs and rock, patches of snow appear and, soon, the cap of the mountain is thick with the white stuff. Up there, rivers no longer flow; they freeze.

WATCH YOUR STEP

While there aren't many plants on the mountains, an occasional tree will sprout up on the lower levels, inviting animals to wander upwards. Sheep, pigs, goats and cows sometimes brave the heights and mobs certainly love the dangerous caves which litter the mountainsides. Danger is everywhere at that height; one wrong step can lead to a fall, especially if running away from creepers or Endermen.

BEAUTY IN NATURE

The mountains are also incredibly beautiful. Waterfalls cascade from gaps in the rocks and sometimes a lava flow can produce volcanic effects. The shapes of the rocks and outcrops of stone can be dramatic. They can be harsh and unforgiving, but mountains provide the most breathtaking views in the Overworld.

MOUNTAIN MISSION

Rosa walks across grass and under trees towards the mountains in front of her. This whole area is full of tall, snow-capped peaks, with a river cutting through at the base. Rosa plans to climb to the very top to investigate, explore and build. As she nears the bottom of the closest mountain, the grass begins to thin, and stone becomes the only solid ground.

REGULAR AND IRREGULAR POLYGONS

Rosa moves quickly to the top of the mountain. The outlines of the rugged landscape she sees below make her think about lots of other straight-sided shapes.

1

Tick the irregular polygons.

2

Draw a suitable polygon in each part of this table.

Polygon	Regular	Irregular
Triangle		
Quadrilateral		
Hexagon		

3

Sketch an irregular polygon with two acute angles and two obtuse angles.

COLOUR IN HOW MANY EMERALDS YOU EARNED

2-D SHAPES

Rosa thinks of lots of shapes, wondering which she could use in construction. She sketches them so she can see what they would look like when seen from above.

1

Look at these shapes Rosa has drawn.

Hexagon   **Rectangle**   **Triangle**   **Rhombus**   **Irregular hexagon**

   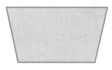

Parallelogram   **Circle**   **Pentagon**   **Octagon**   **Trapezium**

Which shape has the most:

a)   lines of symmetry?   ....

b)   right angles?   ....

c)   pairs of parallel lines?   ....

d)   vertices?   ....

2

Sketch four different shapes that you could make by joining these triangles together.

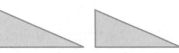

3

How many isosceles triangles are needed to make an octagon?
You can use the space to draw an octagon to help you.

....

4

What is the smallest number of triangles needed to make a rhombus?
You can use the space to draw a rhombus to help you.

....

5

Which 2-D shape has:

a)   6 straight edges? ....   b)   no straight edges? ....

3-D SHAPES

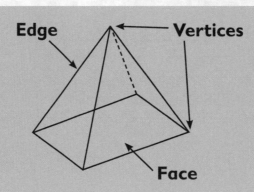

Edge — Vertices

Face

Rosa remembers that she has seen some interesting 3-D shapes in a book. She thinks they make lovely shapes for sculptures. See if you can help her to identify some of their properties.

1

Name these 3-D shapes.

a)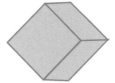

....

b)

....

c)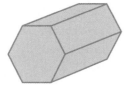

....

d)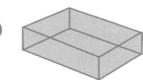

....

e)

....

f)

....

2

How many triangular faces does a square-based pyramid have? ....

Standing on the mountain top enables Rosa to appreciate the landscape in a much different way. It inspires her with all sorts of new construction ideas. Answer more questions to help to improve her knowledge of 3-D shapes.

3

Complete this table for a pentagonal prism.

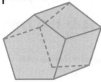

Number of edges	Number of faces	Number of vertices

4

Name these 3-D shapes:

a) A prism with 5 faces, 9 edges and 6 vertices ....

b) A pyramid with 7 faces, 12 edges and 7 vertices ....

5

 Here is a shape made from six blocks:

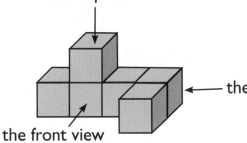

the top view

the side view

the front view

Sketch the shape as if you were looking at it from:

a) the top view   b) the side view   c) the front view

PROPERTIES OF RECTANGLES

To the north, Rosa can see a glowing light coming from behind a small group of rocks. As she gets closer, she can see lava spilling from the mountain. The lava is pouring into a rectangular crater, creating a pool. Rosa throws in a block of cobblestone and watches it burn away.

1

What do the angles in a rectangle add up to in degrees? .... °

2

Here is a rectangular lava pool.

Colour the pairs of parallel sides in different colours.

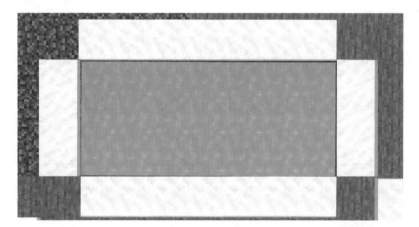

3

Circle **True** or **False** for each statement.

a) A rectangle is a 3-D shape.   **True / False**

b) A rectangle has four equal angles.   **True / False**

c) A rectangle is a quadrilateral.   **True / False**

d) A rectangle has four acute angles.   **True / False**

e) All prisms have some rectangular faces.   **True / False**

f) All pyramids have some rectangular faces. **True / False**

As Rosa climbs over a stone outcrop, she spots a llama stuck on some rock in a bigger pool of lava. She must save the llama by building across to it. Llamas are very helpful animals – once they are tamed, they can be equipped with a chest to carry around. Rosa cannot saddle the llama, but she will guide it with a lead.

4

Here is a picture of the larger lava pool.

Find the two lengths labelled *a* and *b* in this picture.

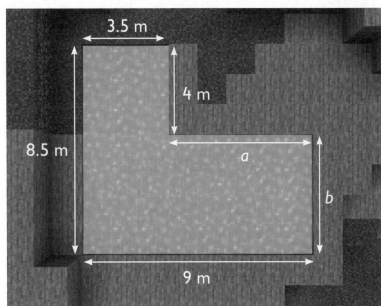

a = ... m   *b* = ... m

5

a) Accurately draw a rectangle with length 4 cm and width 3 cm.

b) Measure the length of one diagonal of your rectangle.   .... cm

ANGLES

Rosa and her llama are trying to find a safe way to climb down the mountain. Usually, Rosa would jump off into a pool of water or a river, but she can't do that with the llama following. Rosa uses her knowledge of angles to find a safe route down the steep slopes.

1

Write these angle types in order of size from largest to smallest:

right angle   **obtuse angle**   **acute angle**   **reflex angle**

....

2

Tick the angle that is a reflex angle.

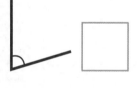 ☐    ☐   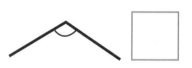 ☐

 ☐    ☐

3

How many degrees does the minute hand of a clock rotate through in one hour?

°

....

Around halfway down the mountain, Rosa stops to do some mining. Emeralds are usually found inside mountains. As Rosa breaks a block of stone, she realises she is taking damage. Ouch! There are no mobs near her as she has made a tunnel but, at her feet, she notices silverfish coming at her from all angles.

 4

Draw lines to join each marked angle to its measurement in degrees.

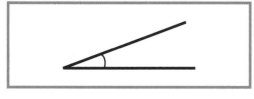

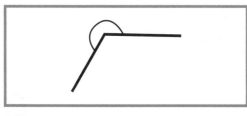

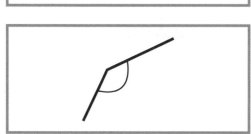

75°

150°

250°

25°

 5

Which two of these angles put together would make an obtuse angle?

A    B   C 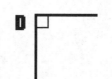   D   E

.... and ....

CALCULATING ANGLES

The silverfish are hard to hit because they are so small. Rosa is not sure if searching for emeralds is worth all this trouble. She eventually decides to stop mining.

1

Find the angles marked ? in these right angles.

a)

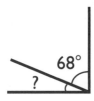

68°

?

..........................°

b) 11°

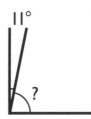

?

..........................°

2

Find the angles marked ? on these straight lines.

a)

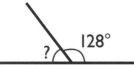

? 128°

..........................°

b)

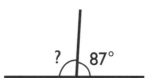

? 87°

..........................°

From looking out of the tunnel Rosa has dug, it seems to be getting dark. It's later than she thought and mobs will be out soon. While she prepares to walk home, work out these angle problems.

3

How many degrees does the hour hand on a clock move through from 13:00 to 17:00?

°
....

4

Work out the size of each angle marked ? in these diagrams.

a)

189°

?

°
....

b)

36° 71°
?

°
....

5

 Angle *a* and angle *b* are equal.

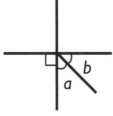

b

a

Work out the size of angle *b*.

°
....

CO-ORDINATES

::

Rosa reaches the bottom of the mountains, only to find four mobs waiting for her. With her sword ready, she goes on the attack. She slices the zombie, whacks the skeleton, swings at the spider, and knocks out the creeper.

1

a) Plot the points with the following co-ordinates on the grid. They show the positions of the mobs.

(3, 5)　　(4, 9)　　(5, 5)　　(6, 9)

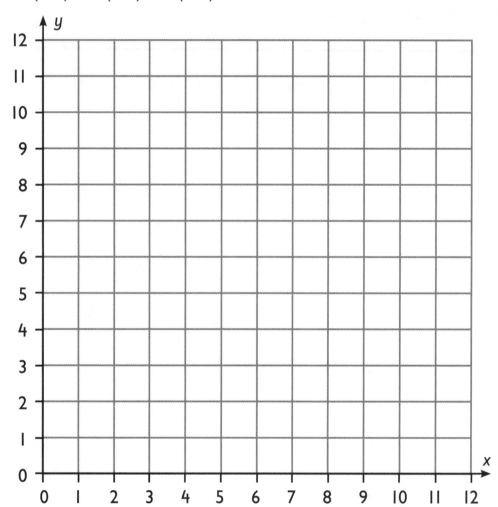

b) The points are the four vertices of a shape.

Name the shape. ....

Rosa can't see any more mobs but she can hear a zipping sound, which can only be an Enderman teleporting back and forth. Rosa spins in a circle trying to spot the Enderman and land an attack. Even the llama is spitting to try to damage this enemy!

2

The llama is standing at the point exactly halfway between (2, 4) and (2, 10).

What are the co-ordinates of this point?   (..................., ...)

3

Three vertices of a square are: (1, 5)   (4, 5)   (1, 8)

The Enderman is at the missing vertex of this square.

Write the co-ordinates of the point where the Enderman is, so Rosa can attack it.

(..................., ...)

4

 The vertices of a rectangle are: (7, 6)   (3, 6)   (3, 8)   (7, 8)

This rectangle is drawn on a 1 cm grid.

Work out the perimeter of the rectangle.   .... cm

COLOUR IN HOW MANY EMERALDS YOU EARNED

TRANSLATION

The Enderman goes down, leaving an Ender pearl behind. Rosa pockets the pearl, knowing she'll need it later in her adventure. Grabbing the lead for the llama, she makes a dash for it and runs in the direction of home.

I

From a distance, Rosa spots what might be the roof of her house.

Draw the translation of this shape 3 squares left and 2 squares up.

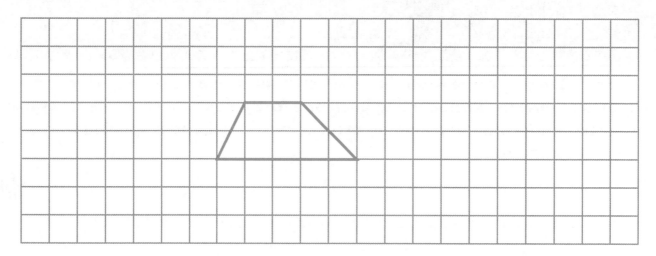

Rosa throws open the front door, pulling her llama in with her. But she is not alone in her house, plus all of her furniture has been moved around! She can hear someone in the next room and she can hear her wolf yapping. This is definitely not a robber; it can only be one person...

2

Shapes 1, 2, 3, 4 and 5 are identical rectangles. They show how one of Rosa's tables has been moved from one place to another.

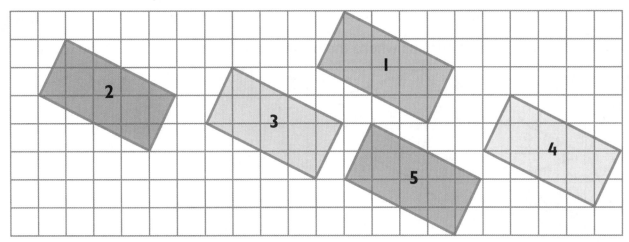

Describe the translation that takes:

a) shape 1 to shape 3 ....

b) shape 2 to shape 5 ....

c) shape 4 to shape 2. ....

3

Rosa tries to work out what's happening in the next room.

She draws a point at co-ordinates (7, 12) on a grid. She translates the point 3 squares right and 2 squares down.

What are the new co-ordinates of the point? (............, ...)

4

 After a translation 4 right and 8 up, the vertices of a shape are at:
(11, 10)   (12, 13)   (14, 10)   (9, 13)
Find the co-ordinates of the vertices **before** the translation.

(............, ...) (............, ...) (............, ...) (............, ...)

REFLECTION

Phew! It's only Isaac. He stopped by for a visit and was just playing with the wolf until she arrived back home. Rosa excitedly tells him about her mountain adventure. While she reflects on her travels, carry out some reflections of your own – of a mathematical kind!

1

Circle the letters for the diagrams where the bottom shape is a reflection of the top shape.

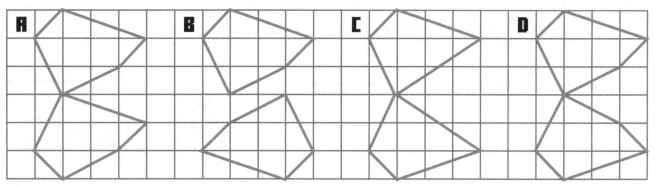

2

Draw the reflection of this shape in the mirror line.

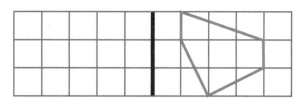

3

Draw the reflection of this shape in the mirror line.

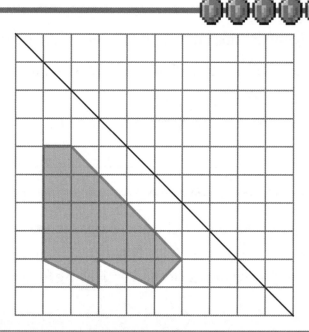

COLOUR IN HOW MANY EMERALDS YOU EARNED

ADVENTURE ROUND-UP

INSPIRING LANDSCAPE

What an interesting day Rosa has had! She set out at the start of the day to explore some mountains, hoping to find some interesting materials. Instead, she took inspiration from the geometry of her spectacular surroundings to come up with some creative ideas.

LLAMA TO LEND A HAND

Finding a llama friend was a lovely surprise. Rosa will let the llama stay inside the house for tonight and first thing tomorrow she will build it a cosy barn. The next time Rosa goes out to collect materials, she will definitely take the llama along to help carry everything back home.

SAFETY FIRST

Of course, it wouldn't be a proper expedition without bumping into some dangerous mobs. But Rosa knows how to handle them and while she may be worried, she knows that staying calm and thinking clearly leads to the best outcome. The silverfish were a nuisance. Rather than continuing to fight when she got tired, Rosa knew the safest thing to do was to leave for home. One day she will return to the mountains and mine all the emeralds she can!

STATISTICS

PEACE OF THE PLAINS

The plains are reasonably peaceful and are where our heroes have their permanent homes. The sounds of animals come from the farm behind Isaac's house. The sun stretches across the open fields between groups of trees. Mobs from the previous night are staggering around, searching for shade.

QUIVER IN THE RIVER

The grass of the plains is always a deep green, often fed by rivers winding through the creases of the land. Deep within these rivers are flashes of salmon and the occasional squid, dashing away from the drowned which shake their tridents at being disturbed. The drowned tug at the ankles of swimmers, hoping to nibble on toes.

A NEW DEVELOPMENT

After his adventures in the savanna and the swamp, Isaac has returned to familiar territory. He is back in the plains but has seen something that wasn't there before. It's a tall structure. Deciding to investigate, Isaac puts on his armour and grabs his sword and bow.

TABLES AND TIMETABLES

As Isaac walks across the plains, the shape in the distance starts becoming clearer. It's a tower, made of stone and dark wood. Banners of grey faces hang from the walls, scarecrows stand nearby with arrows stuck in them, and an iron golem is caged up a little way from the tower. Isaac creeps closer to investigate.

 I

Isaac can see signs next to the scarecrows. It looks like whoever lives here was having an archery competition. This table shows the number of points each person scored for each target.

	Archer A	Archer B	Archer C	Archer D
Target 1	89	96	103	101
Target 2	102	100	110	106
Target 3	106	101	115	122
Target 4	110	121	98	98
Target 5	119	119	119	99
Target 6	101	101	89	95
Target 7	92	107	113	124

a) Who had the highest score on target 4? ....

b) On target 6, which archer scored 95? ....

c) i) What is the highest score in the table? ....

ii) Who was this, and on which target? ....

d) Who had the highest score over the seven targets? ....

e) What is the difference between the highest and the lowest scores on target 7? ....

It's a pillager outpost! This is quite something! At this tower, pillagers gather and plan their raids on nearby villages.

2

This table shows the types of food stolen across five days.

	Day 1	Day 2	Day 3	Day 4	Day 5	Total
Apples	25		22	24	28	131
Carrots				25	27	169
Potatoes	12	18	11	9	12	
Total	73	95	69		67	362

a) How many potatoes were stolen in total? ....

b) How many carrots were stolen on day 3? ....

c) How many apples were stolen on day 2? ....

d) How many pieces of food were stolen on day 4? ....

3

The angry pillagers have stolen lots of items from villager chests. This frequency table shows the total number of items stolen from different villagers.

	Number of items stolen from villager	Frequency
Cartographer		37
Weaponsmith	JHT JHT JHT JHT JHT JHT JHT JHT I	
Butcher		45
Librarian	JHT JHT JHT JHT JHT JHT JHT JHT II	
Shepherd	JHT JHT JHT III	
Farmer		29
Stone mason	JHT JHT JHT JHT JHT JHT JHT IIII	
Fisherman		32

a) Complete the frequency table.

b) Which villager had fewest items stolen? ....

c) How many items were stolen in total? ....

d) Which villager had most items stolen? .... By how many? ....

Isaac dashes behind a tree as he hears pillagers leaving the tower. He doesn't want to be seen as these enemies will attack him straight away. Watching them closely, he can see they walk routes around the tower, keeping guard. His aim is to free the iron golem, but he must wait for a gap in the patrol. Isaac records the patrols in a timetable.

4

This timetable shows when six pillager guards (A, B, C, D, E and F) pass five numbered landmarks (1, 2, 3, 4 and 5) on their patrol route. Some of the guards pass all the landmarks but others only pass some of them.

	Guard A	Guard B	Guard C	Guard D	Guard E	Guard F
Landmark 1	09:45	10:18	10:51	11:18	11:45	12:18
Landmark 2	---	10:31	---	11:31	---	12:31
Landmark 3	10:16	10:48	11:22	11:50	12:17	12:49
Landmark 4	10:33	11:04	---	12:04	---	13:04
Landmark 5	10:45	11:16	11:54	12:17	12:43	13:15

a) How many of the guards pass Landmark 2 on their patrol? ....

b) Isaac spied on Landmark 3 at five minutes to 11.

At what time did a guard next pass Landmark 3 on their patrol? ....

c) Isaac watched over Landmark 4 at midday and saw the next guard arrive there.

At what time did that guard reach Landmark 5 on their patrol? ....

d) Isaac got in position to spy on Landmark 5 at half-past twelve.

Which guard did he next see on patrol at Landmark 5? ....

e) Isaac was hiding close to Landmark 1 at half-past nine.

How many minutes passed before a guard appeared at Landmark 1 whose route included Landmark 2? ....

f) How long in minutes does the patrol from Landmark 2 to Landmark 4 take? ....

BAR CHARTS

Isaac waits and waits. When the time is right, he runs over to the cage and chops at the bars with his axe. The golem is free! While the pillagers are distracted in battle with the iron golem, Isaac finds a book with details of their village raids.

1

This bar chart shows how many items were stolen by four pillagers in raids on five villages.

a) How many items did pillager 2 steal in Happy Hills?

b) Which pillager stole the most number of items in Farming Fields?

c) Which pillager stole the most number of items in total?

d) From which village did pillager 3 steal most items?

e) Which two villages lost most items to every pillager?

and

f) What was the difference in the number of items stolen by pillager 4 in Quiet Corner and Sleepy Village?

g) Which village lost fewest items to all four pillagers?

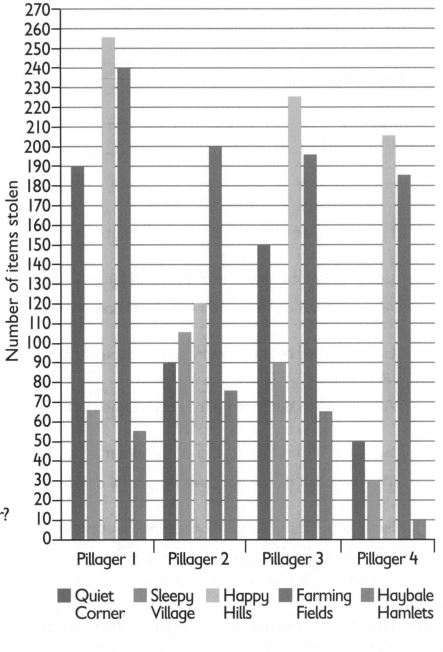

Pillager raids on five villages

Isaac enters the tower while the iron golem fights the pillagers outside. He dodges an arrow whizzing through the air and sees a pillager at the top of the stairs ahead. Isaac defeats the pillager and finds a chest that is full of ore and other items stolen from the nearby village.

2

The table shows the number of different ores that Isaac discovers.

Ore	Number of ore
Iron	35
Gold	25
Redstone	60
Lapis lazuli	45

Draw a bar chart to show this information.

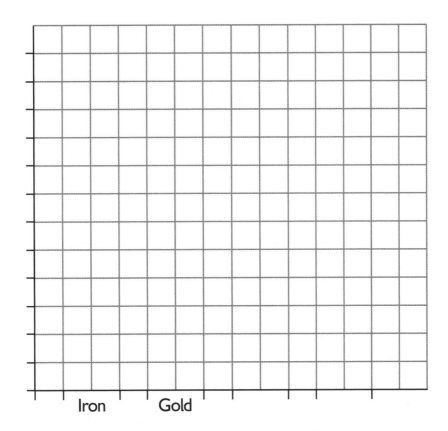

Iron   Gold

LINE GRAPHS

The battle is won! With the iron golem beside him, Isaac walks into the local village to return the stolen possessions he has retrieved from the pillager outpost. It's getting late, so he stays overnight and makes plans to celebrate his victory with a picnic and a spot of fishing in the morning.

 I

This line graph compares the temperature inside and outside a house during the day.

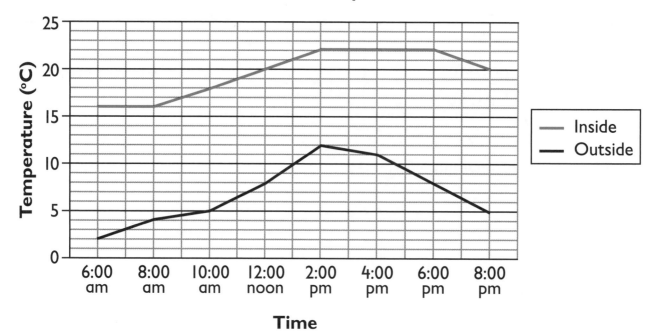

Inside and outside temperature

— Inside
— Outside

a)   What was the temperature outside at 10 am?   ....°C

b)   What was the difference in temperature outside at 6 am and 6 pm?   ....°C

c)   For how long was the inside temperature above 20°C?   .... hours

d)   What was the difference between the inside and outside
temperatures at 4 pm?   .... °C

COLOUR IN HOW MANY EMERALDS YOU EARNED

ADVENTURE ROUND-UP

GOLEM ON GUARD

When Isaac gets up in the morning, he makes himself a picnic and walks to a nearby lake. He enjoys a successful fishing session before starting the journey home. As Isaac reaches the outskirts, he looks back and sees the iron golem begin its patrol of the village. He's happy that everyone there is safe again.

ANSWERS

Pages 5–7

1. a) 97,893   [1 emerald]
   b) 129,087   [1 emerald]
   c) 779,952   [1 emerald]
2. a) 79,497   [1 emerald]
   b) 79,506   [1 emerald]
   c) 79,596   [1 emerald]
   d) 80,496   [1 emerald]
   e) 89,496   [1 emerald]
   f) 179,496   [1 emerald]
3. a) 51,627   [1 emerald]
   b) Twenty thousand and forty-six   [1 emerald]
4. 39,184   [1 emerald]
5. a) >   [1 emerald]
   b) <   [1 emerald]
6. a) Thirty (30)   [1 emerald]
   b) Forty thousand (40,000)   [1 emerald]
   c) Five thousand (5,000)   [1 emerald]
7. The following boxes should be coloured in:
   1,392,482; 37,476; 583,406.87   [1 emerald each]
8. a) 800,000   [1 emerald]
   b) 800,000   [1 emerald]
9. a) 70,000 − 20,000 = 50,000   [1 emerald]
   b) 70,000 + 40,000 = 110,000   [1 emerald]
10. a) 34,999   [1 emerald]
    b) 25,000   [1 emerald]

Pages 8–9

1. a) 77   [1 emerald]
   b) 109   [1 emerald]
   c) 655   [1 emerald]
2. Roman numerals joined to numbers as follows:
   CXLV to 145   [1 emerald]
   CCXX to 220   [1 emerald]
   XCVI to 96   [1 emerald]
   CDIX to 409   [1 emerald]
   CXXII to 122   [1 emerald]
3. 2014   [1 emerald]
4. a) DCLX   [1 emerald]
   b) XXII   [1 emerald]
   c) CLXXII   [1 emerald]
5. a) CX   [1 emerald]
   b) XCVIII   [1 emerald]
   c) DCCCIX   [1 emerald]
   d) CCL   [1 emerald]
   e) CCLXX   [1 emerald]

Pages 10–11

1. a) 3°C   [1 emerald]
   b) 0°C   [1 emerald]
   c) −3°C   [1 emerald]
2. a) 2   [1 emerald]
   b) −8   [1 emerald]
3. a) −3   [1 emerald]
   b) −2   [1 emerald]
4. Layer 4   [1 emerald]
5. 3°C   [1 emerald]

Pages 12–13

1. 1 and 24, 2 and 12, 3 and 8, 4 and 6   [2 emeralds for all pairs; 1 emerald for two pairs]
2. Circled: 2, 11, 17   [2 emeralds for all correct; 1 emerald for two correct]
3. a) 25   [1 emerald]
   b) 8   [1 emerald]
   c) 100   [1 emerald]
4. 3   [1 emerald]
5. a) 12   [1 emerald]
   b) 24   [1 emerald]
   c) 18   [1 emerald]
   d) 28   [1 emerald]
6. 83, 89   [1 emerald]
7. 36 and 64   [1 emerald]

Page 14

1. 200,000   [1 emerald]
2. 13°C   [1 emerald]
3. 1912   [1 emerald]
4. 9 and 16   [1 emerald]

Pages 17–19

1. a) 61,000   [1 emerald]
   b) 69,100   [1 emerald]
   c) 110,300   [1 emerald]
   d) 1,005   [1 emerald]
2. a) 45,972   [1 emerald]
   b) 41,110   [1 emerald]
3. a) 2,702   [1 emerald]
   b) 10,014   [1 emerald]
   c) 2,092   [1 emerald]
   d) 9,373   [1 emerald]
4. 6,000 + 3,000 + 14,000 = 23,000   [1 emerald]
5. a) 112,961   [1 emerald]
   b) 686,144   [1 emerald]
6. a) 6,389 + 2,584 = 8,973   [1 emerald]
   b) 7,083 − 2,479 = 4,604   [1 emerald]

7 **a)** 70,000 − 20,000 = 50,000 [1 emerald]
   b) 80,000 + 50,000 = 130,000 [1 emerald]
   c) 90,000 − 70,000 = 20,000 [1 emerald]
   d) 10,000 + 20,000 = 30,000 [1 emerald]
8 10,388 − 6,178 − 1,894 [1 emerald]
   = 2,316 wooden planks [1 emerald]

Pages 20–21

1 **a)** Cali [1 emerald]
   b) 25,165 [1 emerald]
2 20,569 − 3,029 [1 emerald]
   = 17,540 seats [1 emerald]
3 5,245 + 2,789 + 750 − 2,144 − 378 [1 emerald]
   = 6,262 books [1 emerald]
4 125,000 − 30,000 − 8,000 [1 emerald]
   = 87,000 paper [1 emerald]
5 22,000 − 3,835 − 4,087 − 7,266 [1 emerald]
   = 6,812 books [1 emerald]

Pages 22–23

1 **a)** 3,700 sugar cane [1 emerald]
   b) 9,460 paper [1 emerald]
   c) 23,000 leather [1 emerald]
   d) 600 glass bottles [1 emerald]
   e) 6,000 Nether wart [1 emerald]
   f) 36,000 gunpowder [1 emerald]
2 **a)** 864 [1 emerald]
   b) 1,428 [1 emerald]
   c) 11,825 [1 emerald]
   d) 109,890 [1 emerald]
3 **a)** 4,320 [1 emerald]
   b) 1,500 [1 emerald]
4 **a)** 6,578 × 4 = 26,312 [1 emerald]
   b) 2,487 × 6 = 14,922 [1 emerald]
5 **a)** 85 × 76 (= 6,460) [1 emerald]
   b) 5 × 678 (= 3,390) [1 emerald]

Pages 24–25

1 **a)** 15,600 potatoes [1 emerald]
   b) 7 carrots [1 emerald]
   c) 60 beetroot [1 emerald]
2 **a)** 248 pumpkin pie [1 emerald]
   b) 105 cookies [1 emerald]
   c) 56 cocoa beans [1 emerald]
   d) 1,711 eggs [1 emerald]
   e) 633 wheat [1 emerald]
   f) 686 sugar [1 emerald]
3 **a)** 1,248 [1 emerald]
   b) 984 [1 emerald]
4 **a)** 2,248 ÷ 4 = 562 [1 emerald]
   b) 5,274 ÷ 6 = 879 [1 emerald]
5 3 diamonds [1 emerald]

Page 26

1 3 × 750 = 2,250 [1 emerald]
   2,250 ÷ 7 = 321 (full sets of) leggings [1 emerald]
2 1,176 × 8 ÷ 7 [1 emerald]
   = 1,344 [1 emerald]
3 Any suitable answer from: 12 stacks have 4 helmets and 1 stack has 5 helmets; 2 stacks have 4 helmets and 9 stacks have 5 helmets; 7 stacks have 4 helmets and 5 stacks have 5 helmets. [1 emerald]

Page 29

1 **a)** $\frac{1}{3} = \frac{2}{6}$ [1 emerald]
   b) $\frac{3}{4} = \frac{9}{12}$ [1 emerald]
   c) $\frac{10}{12} = \frac{5}{6}$ [1 emerald]
2 **a)** $\frac{1}{10} = \frac{2}{20} = \frac{3}{30}$ [1 emerald]
   b) $\frac{2}{3} = \frac{4}{6} = \frac{8}{12}$ [1 emerald]
3 Any suitable answers. For example:
   $\frac{2}{4}$ $\frac{3}{6}$ $\frac{4}{8}$ [1 emerald each]

Pages 30–31

1 Mixed numbers joined to improper fractions as follows: $4\frac{3}{5}$ to $\frac{23}{5}$; $8\frac{2}{10}$ to $\frac{82}{10}$; $6\frac{4}{5}$ to $\frac{34}{5}$; $8\frac{2}{9}$ to $\frac{74}{9}$; $2\frac{1}{3}$ to $\frac{7}{3}$; $2\frac{2}{3}$ to $\frac{8}{3}$; $\frac{8}{4}$ to 2 [1 emerald each]
2 **a)** $2\frac{1}{2} = \frac{5}{2}$ [1 emerald]
   b) $3\frac{2}{5} = \frac{17}{5}$ [1 emerald]
   c) $4\frac{5}{8} = \frac{37}{8}$ [1 emerald]
3 **a)** $\frac{7}{2} = 3\frac{1}{2}$ [1 emerald]
   b) $\frac{11}{3} = 3\frac{2}{3}$ [1 emerald]
   c) $\frac{23}{10} = 2\frac{3}{10}$ [1 emerald]
4 $3\frac{1}{12}$ [1 emerald]
5 $\frac{403}{6}$ [1 emerald]

Pages 32–33

1 **a)** $\frac{4}{6}$ [1 emerald]
   b) $\frac{7}{12}$ [1 emerald]
   c) $\frac{7}{8}$ [1 emerald]
2 **a)** $\frac{4}{10}$ [1 emerald]
   b) $\frac{1}{3}$ [1 emerald]
   c) $\frac{3}{8}$ [1 emerald]
3 **a)** < [1 emerald]
   b) > [1 emerald]
   c) > [1 emerald]
4 **a)** $\frac{11}{15}$ [1 emerald]
   b) $\frac{4}{5}$ [1 emerald]
   c) $\frac{5}{12}$ [1 emerald]
5 **a)** $\frac{13}{20}$ [1 emerald]
   b) $\frac{2}{3}$ [1 emerald]

Pages 34–35

1 **a)** $\frac{3}{5}$ [1 emerald]
   b) $\frac{7}{10}$ [1 emerald]
   c) $\frac{1}{3}$ [1 emerald]
   d) $\frac{3}{4}$ [1 emerald]
   e) $\frac{3}{10}$ [1 emerald]

f) $\frac{2}{6}$ (or $\frac{1}{3}$)   [1 emerald]

2 a) $\frac{12}{8}$ (or $\frac{6}{4}$ or $\frac{3}{2}$)   [1 emerald]

  b) $\frac{12}{7}$ [1 emerald]

  c) $\frac{5}{3}$ [1 emerald]

  d) $\frac{5}{4}$ [1 emerald]

3 a) $1\frac{2}{5}$ [1 emerald]

  b) $1\frac{3}{12}$ (or $1\frac{1}{4}$)   [1 emerald]

  c) $1\frac{5}{7}$ [1 emerald]

  d) $7\frac{2}{3}$ [1 emerald]

4 $\frac{5}{12}$ [1 emerald]

5 a) $\frac{8}{12}$ [1 emerald]

  b) $\frac{5}{3}$ [1 emerald]

  c) $\frac{3}{4}$ [1 emerald]

Pages 36–37

1 a) 6.245, 6.254, 6.452, 6.542   [1 emerald]

  b) 11.018, 11.081, 11.1, 11.18   [1 emerald]

2 a) 6   [1 emerald]

  b) 12   [1 emerald]

  c) 219   [1 emerald]

  d) 5,727   [1 emerald]

3 Run 1   [1 emerald]

4 a) 7.1   [1 emerald]

  b) 25.6   [1 emerald]

  c) 4.0   [1 emerald]

  d) 752.2   [1 emerald]

  e) 2,450.7   [1 emerald]

  f) 50,106.9   [1 emerald]

5 Answer: 8.43   [1 emerald]

Explanation: All the other numbers round to 9 to the nearest whole number. 8.43 rounds to 8.   [1 emerald]

Pages 38–39

1 a) 0.25   [1 emerald]

  b) 0.2   [1 emerald]

  c) 0.5   [1 emerald]

  d) 0.4   [1 emerald]

  e) 0.4   [1 emerald]

  f) 0.07   [1 emerald]

2 0.75 kg   [1 emerald]

3 a) 0.08   [1 emerald]

  b) 0.9   [1 emerald]

  c) 0.29   [1 emerald]

  d) 0.439   [1 emerald]

  e) 0.051   [1 emerald]

  f) 0.003   [1 emerald]

4 a) $\frac{7}{10}$ [1 emerald]

  b) $\frac{3}{100}$ [1 emerald]

  c) $\frac{607}{1,000}$ [1 emerald]

  d) $\frac{501}{1,000}$ [1 emerald]

  e) $\frac{97}{1,000}$ [1 emerald]

  f) $\frac{777}{1,000}$ [1 emerald]

5 a) Any decimal number 0.29 or less   [1 emerald]

  b) Any decimal number 0.74 or less   [1 emerald]

c) Any decimal number 0.16 or greater   [1 emerald]

d) Any decimal number 0.27 or less   [1 emerald]

Pages 40–41

1 a) $\frac{5}{100}$ (or $\frac{1}{20}$)   [1 emerald]

  b) $\frac{29}{100}$ [1 emerald]

  c) $\frac{43}{100}$ [1 emerald]

  d) $\frac{87}{100}$ [1 emerald]

2 a) 0.09   [1 emerald]

  b) 0.5   [1 emerald]

  c) 0.67   [1 emerald]

  d) 0.99   [1 emerald]

3 a) 57%   [1 emerald]

  b) 30%   [1 emerald]

  c) 1%   [1 emerald]

  d) 13%   [1 emerald]

  e) 25%   [1 emerald]

  f) 90%   [1 emerald]

4 Bottles joined as follows:

$\frac{3}{10}$ to 30%; 100% to $\frac{10}{10}$; $\frac{3}{50}$ to 6%; 0.2 to 20%; 60% to 0.6; 0.01 to 1%; 85% to $\frac{85}{100}$; 0.4 to $\frac{2}{5}$ [1 emerald each]

5 80% of the zombie equals $\frac{4}{5}$ of its 20 sections

                 [1 emerald]

$\frac{4}{5}$ of 20 = 16   [1 emerald]

Pages 42–43

1 a) $\frac{4}{3} = 1\frac{1}{3}$ [1 emerald]

  b) $\frac{8}{3} = 2\frac{2}{3}$ [1 emerald]

  c) $\frac{6}{3} = 2$ [1 emerald]

2 a) $\frac{9}{5} = 1\frac{4}{5}$ [1 emerald]

  b) $\frac{8}{5} = 1\frac{3}{5}$ [1 emerald]

3 a) $\frac{6}{12}$ or $\frac{1}{2}$ [1 emerald]

  b) $\frac{5}{4}$ [1 emerald]

  c) $\frac{9}{4}$ [1 emerald]

  d) $\frac{8}{4}$ or 2   [1 emerald]

4 a) $\frac{6}{2}$ or 3   [1 emerald]

  b) $\frac{3}{6}$ or $\frac{1}{2}$ [1 emerald]

  c) $\frac{15}{12}$ or $\frac{5}{4}$ [1 emerald]

5 a) $5\frac{2}{4}$ or $5\frac{1}{2}$ [1 emerald]

  b) $8\frac{1}{4}$ [1 emerald]

  c) $8\frac{3}{4}$ [1 emerald]

Page 44

1 40%   [1 emerald]

2 $4\frac{1}{2}$ litres   [1 emerald]

3 $\frac{3}{8} + \frac{1}{4} = \frac{3}{8} + \frac{2}{8} = \frac{5}{8}$ [1 emerald]

$1 - \frac{5}{8} = \frac{3}{8}$ [1 emerald]

Pages 47–49

1 a) 6,000 g   [1 emerald]

  b) 4 l   [1 emerald]

  c) 3,000 kg   [1 emerald]

  d) 7,000 m   [1 emerald]

  e) 50 cm   [1 emerald]

  f) 50 mm   [1 emerald]

2 17 m [1 emerald]

3 The second chest should be ticked [1 emerald]

4 **a)** 3.55 kg [1 emerald]

   b) 2.6 kg [1 emerald]

5 **a)** > [1 emerald]

   b) > [1 emerald]

   c) < [1 emerald]

   d) < [1 emerald]

6 **a)** 12.5 [1 emerald]

   b) 1.1 [1 emerald]

   c) 1,350 [1 emerald]

7 **a)** > [1 emerald]

   b) > [1 emerald]

   c) > [1 emerald]

   d) < [1 emerald]

8 48.4 l (accept 48 l) [1 emerald]

Pages 50–51

1 30 m [1 emerald]

2 24 m [1 emerald]

3 26 m [1 emerald]

4 **a)** 74 m [1 emerald]

   b) 84 m [1 emerald]

5 **a)** 11 cm [1 emerald]

   b) 9 cm [1 emerald]

Pages 52–53

1 50 m² [1 emerald]

2 81 m² [1 emerald]

3 20 cm² (count the squares that are more than half inside the shape) [1 emerald]

4 8 cm [1 emerald]

5 Perimeter: 60 cm [1 emerald]

   Area: 190 cm² [1 emerald]

Pages 54–55

1 **a)** 8 cm³ [1 emerald]

   b) 8 cm³ [1 emerald]

   c) 8 cm³ [1 emerald]

   d) 11 cm³ [1 emerald]

2 64 cm³ [1 emerald]

3 60 cm³ [1 emerald]

4 Any suitable estimate between 40 and 80 cm³ [1 emerald]

5 3 cm [1 emerald]

Pages 56–57

1 £64.21 [1 emerald]

2 £168.75 [1 emerald]

3 £12.65 [1 emerald]

4 £33.18 [1 emerald]

5 **a)** £15 [1 emerald]

   b) £7.50 [1 emerald]

Pages 58–59

1 12:20 pm [1 emerald]

2 8 hours = 480 minutes [1 emerald]

   480 ÷ 8 = 60 ingots [1 emerald]

3 19:20 or 7:20 pm [1 emerald]

4 8 hours + $1\frac{1}{2}$ hours + 20 minutes + 5 minutes

   = 9 hours 55 minutes [1 emerald]

   9 hours 55 minutes after 9:45 am is 7:40 pm or 19:40 [1 emerald]

5 Swamp had 15 hours 1 minute; mountains had 10 hours 14 minutes [1 emerald]

   4 hours 47 minutes [1 emerald]

Pages 60–62

1 £3.20 [1 emerald]

2 Volunteer works $4\frac{1}{2}$ hours per week [1 emerald]

   22 hours 30 minutes [1 emerald]

3 260 emeralds [1 emerald]

4 50 m [1 emerald]

5 11 am [1 emerald]

6 15 + 5 + 35 + 5 = 60 minutes [1 emerald]

   2:10 pm (or 14:10) [1 emerald]

7 2 posts (75 cm × 2 = 1.5 m) can be cut from each 2 m piece of wood [1 emerald]

   7 posts needed so 4 pieces of wood are needed, 4 × £16.50 [1 emerald]

   £66 [1 emerald]

8 Length of one side and height of one side = 960 ÷ 2 = 480 cm [1 emerald]

   Length: 360 cm [1 emerald]

Page 65

1 Third and sixth shapes ticked [1 emerald each]

2 Any suitable sketches. Regular polygons should have all sides of equal length and irregular polygons should have at least one side of a different length to the others. The triangles must have three sides, the quadrilaterals must have four sides and the hexagons must have six sides. [1 emerald for each part of the table correctly completed]

3 Any irregular polygon [1 emerald]

   Two acute angles (less than 90 degrees) within the polygon [1 emerald]

   Two obtuse angles (greater than 90 degrees but less than 180 degrees) within the polygon [1 emerald]

Pages 66–67

1 **a)** Circle [1 emerald]

   b) Rectangle [1 emerald]

   c) Octagon [1 emerald]

   d) Octagon [1 emerald]

2 Any four suitable sketches using the given pair of shapes [1 emerald each]

3 8 [I emerald]

4 2 [I emerald]

5 **a)** Hexagon [I emerald]

   b) Circle [I emerald]

Pages 68–69

I **a)** Cube [I emerald]

   b) Cylinder [I emerald]

   c) Hexagonal prism [I emerald]

   d) Cuboid [I emerald]

   e) Triangle-based pyramid
      (or tetrahedron) [I emerald]

   f) Cone [I emerald]

2 4 [I emerald]

3 Number of edges: 15 [I emerald]

   Number of faces: 7 [I emerald]

   Number of vertices: 10 [I emerald]

4 **a)** Triangular prism [I emerald]

   b) Hexagon-based pyramid [I emerald]

5 **a)** [I emerald]

   b) [I emerald]

   c) [I emerald]

Pages 70–71

I 360° [I emerald]

2 The two pairs of parallel lines should be coloured
differently [I emerald each]

3 **a)** False [I emerald]

   b) True [I emerald]

   c) True [I emerald]

   d) False [I emerald]

   e) True [I emerald]

   f) False [I emerald]

4 $a = 5.5$ m, $b = 4.5$ m [I emerald each]

5 **a)** Any rectangle accurately drawn with length 4 cm
and width 3 cm [I emerald each]

   b) 5 cm [I emerald]

Pages 72–73

I reflex angle, obtuse angle, right angle, acute angle
[I emerald]

2

✓

[I emerald]

3 360° [I emerald]

4

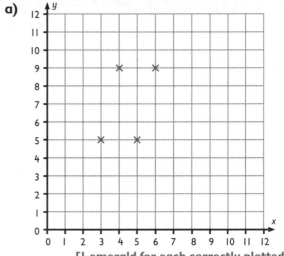

[I emerald each up to a maximum of 3]

5 B and C (or C and D) [I emerald]

Pages 74–75

I **a)** 22° [I emerald]

   b) 79° [I emerald]

2 **a)** 52° [I emerald]

   b) 93° [I emerald]

3 120° [I emerald]

4 **a)** 81° [I emerald]

   b) 73° [I emerald]

5 45° [I emerald]

Pages 76–77

I **a)**

[I emerald for each correctly plotted point]

   b) Parallelogram [I emerald]

2 (2, 7) [I emerald]

3 (4, 8) [I emerald]

4 12 cm [I emerald]

Pages 78–79

I

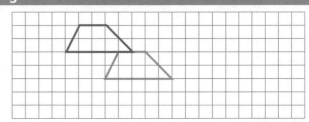

[I emerald for correct translation left;

I emerald for correct translation up]

2 a) 4 squares left and 2 squares down   [1 emerald]
  b) 11 squares right and 3 squares down   [1 emerald]
  c) 16 squares left and 2 squares up   [1 emerald]
3 (10, 10)   [1 emerald]
4 (7, 2)   (8, 5)   (10, 2)   (5, 5)   [1 emerald each]

Page 80

1 C and D circled   [1 emerald each]
2

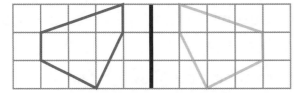

[1 emerald for each correctly reflected side]

3

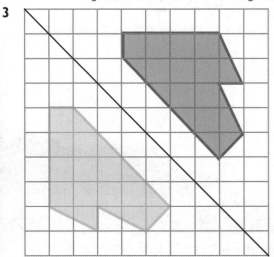

[1 emerald for each correctly reflected side]

Pages 83–85

1 a) Archer B   [1 emerald]
  b) Archer D   [1 emerald]
  c) i) 124   **ii)** Archer D; target 7 [1 emerald each]
  d) Archer C   [1 emerald]
  e) 32   [1 emerald]
2 a) 62   [1 emerald]
  b) 36   [1 emerald]
  c) 32   [1 emerald]
  d) 58   [1 emerald]
3 a) Table completed as follows:

	Number of items stolen from villager	Frequency
Cartographer	𝍠𝍠𝍠𝍠𝍠𝍠𝍠 ‖	37
Weaponsmith	𝍠𝍠𝍠𝍠𝍠𝍠𝍠𝍠 I	41
Butcher	𝍠𝍠𝍠𝍠𝍠𝍠𝍠𝍠𝍠	45
Librarian	𝍠𝍠𝍠𝍠𝍠𝍠𝍠𝍠 ‖	42
Shepherd	𝍠𝍠𝍠 ‖I	18
Farmer	𝍠𝍠𝍠𝍠𝍠 IIII	29
Stone mason	𝍠𝍠𝍠𝍠𝍠𝍠𝍠 IIII	39
Fisherman	𝍠𝍠𝍠𝍠𝍠𝍠 ‖	32

[1 emerald]
  b) Shepherd   [1 emerald]
  c) 283   [1 emerald]

d) Butcher by 3   [1 emerald]
4 a) 3   [1 emerald]
  b) 11:22   [1 emerald]
  c) 12:17   [1 emerald]
  d) Guard E   [1 emerald]
  e) 48 minutes   [1 emerald]
  f) 33 minutes   [1 emerald]

Pages 86–87

1 a) 120   [1 emerald]
  b) Pillager 1   [1 emerald]
  c) Pillager 1   [1 emerald]
  d) Happy Hills   [1 emerald]
  e) Happy Hills and Farming Fields   [1 emerald]
  f) 20   [1 emerald]
  g) Haybale Hamlets   [1 emerald]
2

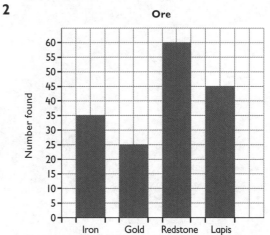

[1 emerald for each correct bar;
1 emerald for axis labels; 1 emerald for title]

Page 88

1 a) 5°C   [1 emerald]
  b) 6°C   [1 emerald]
  c) 8 hours   [1 emerald]
  d) 11°C   [1 emerald]

TRADE IN YOUR EMERALDS!

What an experience that was! Rosa and Isaac ventured far and wide, defeating dangerous mobs and carrying out ambitious building projects. Along the way, you earned emeralds for your hard work. This trader is waiting for you to spend your gems with them. Pretend you're preparing for an adventure that will take you into the ocean. Which items would you want to have with you?

If you have enough emeralds, you could buy more than one of some items.

HMMM?

Write the total number of emeralds you earned in this box:

SHOP INVENTORY

- DIAMOND CHESTPLATE: 30 EMERALDS
- DIAMOND HELMET: 20 EMERALDS
- DIAMOND LEGGINGS: 25 EMERALDS
- ENCHANTED DIAMOND SWORD: 30 EMERALDS
- ENCHANTED TRIDENT: 35 EMERALDS
- SPYGLASS: 15 EMERALDS
- EYE OF ENDER: 10 EMERALDS
- HEART OF THE SEA: 15 EMERALDS
- COOKED COD: 10 EMERALDS
- COOKED SALMON: 15 EMERALDS
- CAKE: 20 EMERALDS
- ENCHANTED GOLDEN APPLE: 30 EMERALDS
- POTION OF REGENERATION: 30 EMERALDS
- POTION OF WATER BREATHING: 25 EMERALDS
- POTION OF NIGHT VISION: 25 EMERALDS

That's a lot of emeralds. Well done! Remember, just like real money, you don't need to spend it all. Sometimes it's good to save up.